SpringerBriefs in Economics

More information about this series at http://www.springer.com/series/8876

Arpita Ghose

Efficiency of Elementary Education in India

Empirical Evidence Using a Nonparametric Data Envelopment Approach

Springer

Arpita Ghose
Department of Economics
Jadavpur University
Kolkata
India

ISSN 2191-5504 ISSN 2191-5512 (electronic)
SpringerBriefs in Economics
ISBN 978-81-322-3659-7 ISBN 978-81-322-3661-0 (eBook)
DOI 10.1007/978-81-322-3661-0

Library of Congress Control Number: 2016952819

Printed on acid-free paper

This Springer imprint is published by Springer Nature
The registered company is Springer (India) Pvt. Ltd.
The registered company address is: 7th Floor, Vijaya Building, 17 Barakhamba Road, New Delhi 110 001, India

Foreword

The present book is a serious effort to measure the efficiency of the school education system in India relative to the spending which is undertaken by the government in different dimensions. The author Arpita Ghose, who has worked extensively on related topics for last few years, has divided the states into general (GCS), special (SCS) and union territory (UT) to understand the outcome of government expenditure in the school education system. The idea of technical efficiency here is simple—how close is the performance of the state compared to the best performer, both within the same category (called the group frontier) and among all the states taken together (called meta-frontier). In other words how good is the school system in terms of some performance index like net enrollment ratio (quantity) and students passing with 60 % marks and above (quality). The inputs used to judge this performance is school per thousand population, teacher–student ratios, etc. Once the degree of inefficiency is found out by Data Envelopment Analysis (DEA), the factors responsible for this like lack of proper infrastructure, location etc are brought into the picture to pinpoint the factor which causes this most.

The book has two great virtues—one is the separation of the states into GCS, SCS and UT for the simple reason that the government spending differs significantly among the category of the states. The other is the application of DEA technique to measure the inefficiency which needs much less restrictions than parametric estimation techniques. The conclusions are also noteworthy in the sense that increase in expenditure alone does not generate either better qualitative outcome or larger quantitative output. In fact, achievement of higher literacy rate or educational development index is not a pre-condition for better efficiency in the school education system in India.

I have no doubt that the painstaking analysis which has gone behind this work will be highly beneficial to researchers, teachers, and students interested in this field. This book will also prove handy to decision makers and policy planners in the government and private sector who are seriously involved with the education sector.

Last but not the least, the book is an outcome of the UGC sponsored UPE programme at Jadavpur University, Kolkata. It gives me great pleasure as joint coordinator of the social science programme under UPE (Phase II) to find that one component of the programme has produced such a nice volume within a short time and the author deserves a special mention for that.

Ajitava Raychaudhuri
Professor and Joint Coordinator
Cultural Resources and Social Science Programme under UPE II
Department of Economics
Jadavpur University
Kolkata, India

Preface

The bulk of the work embodied in this book was undertaken in April 2012 and continued over a period of three years up to September 2015, as the project entitled "Economies of Education", under the group "Cultural Resources and Social Science", under the UGC scheme of "The University with Potential For Excellence". I am deeply indebted to the programme authority for providing the necessary funding to complete the work. I would like to thank Finance Officer of the Jadavpur University for regular release of funds which facilitated the smooth functioning of the project programme and thereby led to the completion of the work as designed. I would also like to thank Prof. Ajitava Raychaudhuri, Professor, Department of Economics, Jadavpur University and Joint Coordinator, Cultural Resources and Social Science Programme under UPE II, for his encouragement, constructive suggestions and support which gave the project the status of a book.

My heartiest thanks to Smt. Amrita Bhanja, Research Assistant of the project for her sincere support.

I owe an intellectual debt to Prof. Subhash Ray, University of Connecticut, USA, whose academic input made it possible to include the Nonparametric Data Envelopment Analysis, as a tool for the measurement of efficiency problem of India's education sector. Discussions with Professor Ray and his constructive criticisms and suggestions were very helpful.

It is not possible to mention the names of all the officials, colleagues, and friends, who contributed and helped during the course of this project. But I would like to mention specifically the encouragement and support given by Dean, Faculty of Arts at Jadavpur University, the coordinators – Prof. M.K. Mitra, Prof. Dipankar Sanyal – of UPE II programme, and Prof. Nilanjana Gupta, Joint coordinator of Cultural Resource and Social Science programme of UPE II, for their support during the project whenever necessary.

Thanks also to honourable Vice-Chancellor and Registrar of Jadavpur University and all the faculty members of the Department of Economics, Jadavpur University, for their co-operation whenever needed. The author would also like to thank the members of Central and Departmental Libraries of Jadavpur University, as well as Library members of Indian Statistical Institute of Kolkata and Delhi Centre, Centre for Studies in Social Science, Kolkata, Bureau of Applied Economics and Statistics Kolkata, Indian Institute of Management Kolkata, and Jawaharlal Nehru University, New Delhi.

The contents of this book is the revised version of the papers presented at the three International conferences: (i) 12th International DEA Conference of International DEA Association, held at Kuala Lumpur, Malaysia, during April 15–17, 2014, (ii) Fourth CESI International Conference, 2013, held at Indian Statistical Institute Kolkata, and organized by Department of Economics, Calcutta University, in association with Indian Statistical Institute Kolkata, Pratichi Institute and Institute of Development Studies Kolkata, during December 28–30, 2013, (iii) the 50th Annual conference of the Indian Econometric Society, organized by Indira Gandhi Institute of Development and Research, Mumbai, during December 22–24, 2013. The earlier version was also presented at a workshop organized by the Department of Economics, Jadavpur University, in April 2013. The suggestions made by the participants of those conferences and the workshop and by Prof. Sarmila Banerjee and Dr. Robindranath Mukherjee of Calcutta University are gratefully acknowledged.

Last but not the least, my gratitude goes to my family members. Though the death of my husband, Dr. Shyamal Kumar Ghose (Professor of Genetics, Head, Department of Genetics, B.C. Agricultural University, West Bengal) is a terrible loss to me, I can visualize his invisible continuous encouragement, extreme patience and moral support, which has sustained me and my work at all times.

Kolkata, India
July 2016

Arpita Ghose

Contents

About the Author

Arpita Ghose is Professor in the Department of Economics, Jadavpur University. She did her Ph.D. from Indian Statistical Institute, Kolkata and works in the area of disequilibrium economics. She has published her research in reputed national and international journals. At present, she is working on computable general equilibrium models, productivity and efficiency analysis using data envelopment approach and stochastic frontier models, and also on applied time series econometrics. She has presented research papers and chaired sessions at different international conferences and symposiums; and completed projects funded by DFID-UNCTAD-Government of India for Jadavpur University's Trade Research Capacity Building Program; Shastri Indo-Canadian Institute, Calgary, Canada; UGC and ICSSR, among others, and has also supervised many Ph.D. students. Her major research areas of interest include econometrics, macroeconomics, economics of social sector and regional development.

Chapter 1
The Background and the Motivation

Abstract The major departure of this book is its approach to estimating technical efficiency (TE) for primary and upper primary education which does not use a single frontier encompassing all the twenty-eight states and seven union territories (UT) over the period 2005–06 to 2010–11, as is done in the available literature. Rather, this method assumes that General Category State (GCS), Special Category States (SCS) &UT are not homogeneous and operate under different fiscal and economic conditions and hence the maximum educational-output producible from an input bundle by a school within a particular group may not be as high as what could be produced if the school could choose to locate in other group. This justifies construction of two group frontiers: (i) for GCS only and (ii) for SCS&UT. The non-parametric Data Envelopment Analysis (DEA) has been used for estimation of TE to see whether in India the schools in different states are technically efficient in the sense that they are generating maximum educational output given the existing resources. The extent of underutilization of different inputs is also estimated. The book also investigates whether the States/UT with high literacy rate and or high educational development index (EDI) are also the States/UT with high technical efficiency. The factors influencing such efficiency are explained separately for the four groups: GCS-primary, GCS upper-primary; SCS&UT-primary and SCS&UT-upper primary highlighting some policy suggestions for improving efficiency. This chapter reports the basic motivation, objectives and the chapter composition of the book.

1.1 Introduction

The development of human capital in an economy is basically dependent on development of education sector. In India's National Development Programme, a substantial emphasis was given to the education sector. Among the different levels of education crucial is the development of elementary level of education which basically builds up the educational backbone of a student. Different programme was launched by the government of India to improve the overall performance of elementary education in India. Elementary Education has been of priority in terms of

A. Ghose, *Efficiency of Elementary Education in India*,
SpringerBriefs in Economics, DOI 10.1007/978-81-322-3661-0_1

sub-sectoral allocations. A number of Schemes like (i) District Primary Education Programme (ii) National Programme of Nutritional Support to Primary Education (Mid-Day Meal Scheme), have been launched by the Central Government to meet the needs of the educationally disadvantaged groups. A comprehensive programme called the Sarva Shiksha Abhijaan (SSA) was launched in November 2000 in partnership with the States. The programme aims to improve the performance of the school system through a community-based approach and to impart quality elementary education to all children in the age group of 6–14 years. It seeks to bridge gender and social disparities at the elementary level. It subsumes all existing programmes, within its overall framework, with the district as the unit level of implementation. National Programme for Education of Girls at the Elementary Level (NPEGEL) has been launched in 2003–04 for providing additional components for education of girls at the Elementary Level under SSA.

Performance of the Education Sector as represented by literacy rate during the Five Year Plan is quite satisfactory. Literacy Rates in India has risen dramatically from 18.3 % in 1951 to 74 % according to provisional census data of 2011. However, vast disparities is present amongst the States regarding Gross Enrolment Ratio at Primary/Upper Primary Level; sates in the North-East performing better than the Other States. Ten States and union territories, including Kerala, Lakshadweep, Mizoram, Tripura, Goa, Daman and Diu, Puducherry, Chandigarh, National Capital Territory of Delhi and the Andaman and Nicobar Islands, have attained literacy rate of above 85 %, the target set by the Planning Commission to be achieved by 2011–12. Kerala has the highest literacy rate at 93.91 % followed by Lakshadweep at 92.28 %. Bihar is at the bottom of the ladder with literacy rate of 63.82 followed by Arunachal Pradesh at 66.95 (http://theonlinegk.wordpress.com/2011/04/02/literacy-rate-in-indian-state-census-2011). In the Indian context some data are available depicting a measure of educational development index (EDI) (Source National University of Educational Planning and Administration, NUEPA). Some of the states and union territories for which EDI is higher than all India level are Andaman and Nicobar Islands, Andhra Pradesh, Chandigarh, Delhi among others for primary level of education and, Karnataka, Kerala, Maharashtra among others, for upper primary level of education. *Given this vast development of the education sector, naturally, a question arises whether the education Sector is functioning efficiently? The related questions are:*

- *Whether the output gets maximized given the quantity of input usage. Here output may be defined as net enrolment ratio and also the student's educational achievement measured by standardized test applied. The question is whether in India the schools in different States are technically efficient in the sense that they are generating maximum output given the existing resources. Is there any room for greater efficiency?*
- *Whether the States/UT with high literacy rate and or high educational development index (EDI) are also the States/UT with high technical efficiency.*
- *Whether the inputs used in the production process are used efficiently?*

- *What are the factors responsible for the variation of technical efficiency across different states of India?*

The present book attempts to answer these above questions.

For attainment of equalization of education facilities across different States of India, an analysis of efficiency at the State level is needed. This will help us to identify the States that are lagging behind with respect to the Indian average in terms of efficiency and also to formulate appropriate policies for enhancing educational efficiency of those States, so that equalization of educational efficiency across different States of India can be ensured.

In efficiency analysis it is not assumed that the production unit always behaves optimally and hence they can operate inefficiently. Efficiency measurement is a two stage problem—In order to judge the performance of the production units, a benchmark production function has to be constructed which is called as frontier, and is supposed to be perfectly efficient. The method of comparing the observed performance of production unit with the postulated standard of perfect efficiency is the basic problem of measuring efficiency.

Research on Efficiency Measurement has, since the seminal work of Farrell (1957) bifurcated, with economists typically following the route of Statistical analysis (Aigner et al. 1977) and management scientists characteristically opting for non-parametric route grounded in linear programming (Charnes et al. 1978). The former approach has come to be known as Stochastic Frontier analysis, the later as Data Envelopment Analysis (DEA) which is basically a linear programming method. Charnes et al. (CCR (1978, 1981)) introduced the method of DEA to address the problem of efficiency measurement for decision making units (DMU) with multiple inputs and multiple outputs. Among the DMU they include non-market agencies like schools, hospitals, courts which produce identifiable and measurable output from measurable inputs but generally lack market prices of outputs (and often some inputs as well) and *constructed a benchmark production function which is called as frontier, and is supposed to be perfectly efficient, using programming approach under the assumption of* constant returns to scale globally. Later Banker et al. (BCC) (1984) extended the CCR model to variable returns to scale. Thus estimation of efficiency score in education basically rests on the assumed input output relationship in education. *The advantage of DEA analysis is that it is not dependent on the prior specification of functional form or the criterion function.*

Several studies have applied DEA in measuring the efficiency and productivity in education sector around the globe. In particular, the technical efficiency of schools was estimated by Ray (1991), Bessent and Bessent (1980), Fare et al. (1989), Bonesrqnning and Rattsq (1994), Jesson et al. (1987) among others.

In the Indian context Tyagi et al. (2009) assessed the technical efficiency and efficiency differences among 348 elementary schools of Uttar Pradesh state in India by using DEA. Sankar (2007) considered efficiency of *elementary education as a whole* for different states of India considering two points of time: the mid-1990s and 2004–05 but not for primary and upper primary level of education separately. In

Sankar (2007) the factors that contribute to the "efficiency scores" largely remain unexplained—However, some of the regressions showed the role of density of population, a proxy to look at concentration factor and hence the scope for economies of scales to operate, as significant. Sengupta and Pal (2010) explained the efficiency *primary education sector in India* using the data provided by District Information System for Education (DISE), National University of Educational Planning and Administration, only for the single year 2005–06. They identified five basic aspects of education: deprivation aspects, social aspects, policy aspects. The country has been divided into five zones: Northern, North-eastern, Eastern, Western and Southern Zone respectively. Using Anand and Sen (1997) formula of Human Poverty Index (HPI) they derived Grand Poverty Index comprising of various poverty indicators of education system in India and tried to relate these with the efficiency score in DEA. The result of their study indicates that poverty indicators have negative impacts on efficiency, whereas social and policy indicators are not significantly related to the efficiency improvement.

1.2 The Objectives of Present Book

The perusal of the literature suggests the following gaps in the existing literature relating to the efficiency of elementary education sector in India.

First of all, while estimating the efficiency score the earlier studies have created the frontier for education output by taking into account all the twenty-eight states and seven union territories in India taken together. The present research departs from this assumption and does not construct a single frontier as not all of them operate under same fiscal and economic environment and hence cannot be taken as homogeneous. Some of the States namely Special Category States (SCS) are given more benefits by the central government like Arunachal Pradesh, Assam, Himachal Pradesh, Jammu and Kashmir, Manipur, Meghalaya, Mizoram, and Nagaland etc. The main reason behind this categorization is the development of that particular state where there are many problems due to hilly terrains, international borders etc. and there cannot be good industrial development. These states have also geographical disadvantages in their effort for infrastructural development. The states in the North-East are also late starters in development. The finances of the state are also less. Thus the central government comes into picture. Public expenditure plays a significant role in the Gross State Domestic Product of the states. 90 % of the central assistance is treated as grant and remaining 10 % is considered as loan unlike other states which get 30 % grant and 70 % loan. The most important prescription for special category states is interest free loan with rationalization of public expenditure based on growth enhancing sectoral allocation of resources. For Special Category States unlike other states there is no hard budget constraint as the central transfer is high. Through the Fiscal Responsibility and Budget Management Act, 2003 (FRBM) these States are also availing themselves of the benefit of debt swapping and debt relief schemes which facilitate reduction of the average annual rate of interest. The union territories (UT) also get more grants as compared to General Category states (GCS). Thus one cannot assume a common frontier for all the States and the union territories as all of them does not belong to the same fiscal and economic environment. It is better to construct two group frontiers: the first one comprising of the states only with GCS and the second one comprising of SCS and UT. This is needed as maximum educational–output producible from an input bundle by a school within a particular group of State may not be as high as what could be produced if the school could choose to locate in other group.

Secondly, although the estimates on technical efficiency score for different states of India at primary level of education are available only for the year 2006, and the technical efficiency score for elementary level of education are available for only the two time points namely the mid-1990s and 2004–05, the figures for the technical efficiency score for the upper primary level of education are practically lacking, so that a comparisons of the efficiency score at primary and upper primary level as well as their temporal variation cannot be made from the earlier studies.

Thirdly, it will be important to measure the extent of underutilization of inputs used in the production process. There is dearth in such measurement for the Indian education sector.

Finally, for policy analysis it is important to know the factors influencing the efficiency of primary and secondary level of education separately and there is a lack of such studies.

The present book attempts to overcome these above limitations and contributes to the literature.

1.3 Arrangements of the Chapters

This chapter Deals with The Background and Motivation of the problems.

Chapter 2 presents an extensive overview of the available methodologies and the existing literature on efficiency of school, higher and further education around the globe including India.

Chapter 3 estimates output oriented measures of technical efficiency and explains its determinants for primary and upper primary level of education of General Category state (GCS), Special Category State (SCS) and Union territories (UT).

Chapter 4 estimates input oriented measures of technical efficiency and explains its determinants for primary and upper primary level of education of General Category state (GCS), Special Category State (SCS) and Union territories (UT).

Chapter 5 presents summary and conclusions and gives some policy suggestions for improving technical efficiency of education.

References

Aigner DJ, Lovell CAK, Schmidt PJ (1977) Formulation and estimation of stochastic frontier production function models. J Econ 6(1):21–37

Anand S, Sen A (1997) Concepts of human development and poverty: a multidimensional perspective. In: Poverty and human development: human development papers 1997, pp. 1–20. United Nations Development Programme, New York

Banker RD, Charnes A, Cooper WW (1984) Some models for estimating technical and scale efficiencies in data envelopment analysis. Manag Sci 30(9):1078–1092

Bessent AM, Bessent EW (1980) Determining the comparative efficiency of schools through data envelopment analysis. Educ Admin Q 16(2):57–75

Bonesronning H, Rattsq J (1994) Efficiency variation among Norwegian high schools: consequences of equalization policy. Econ Educ Rev 3(4):289–304

Charnes A, Cooper WW, Rhodes E (1978) Measuring the efficiency of decision making units. Eur J Oper Res 2(6):429–444

Charnes A, Cooper WW, Rhodes E (1981) Evaluating program and managerial efficiency: an application of DEA to program follow-through. Manag Sci 27(6):668–697

Farrell MJ (1957) The measurement of productive efficiency. J Roy Stat Soc 120(3):253–281

Fare R, Grosskopf S, Weder WL (1989) Measuring school district performance. Public Financ Q 17(4):409–428

Jesson D, Mayston D, Smith P (1987) Performance assessment in the educational sector: educational and economic perspectives. Oxford Rev Educ 13(3):249–266

Ray SC (1991) Resource-use efficiency in public schools: a study of Connecticut data. Manag Sci 37(12):1620–1628

Sankar D (2007) Education system performance among Indian states: a public expenditure efficiency analysis using linear programming methods. Washington DC, World Bank. http://documents.worldbank.org/curated/en/2007/01/8933943/education-system-performance-among-indian-states-public-expenditure-efficiency-analysis-using-linear-programming-methods

Sengupta A, Pal NP (2010) Primary education in India: delivery and outcome- a district level analysis based on DISE data. J Educ Plann Admin 24(1):5–21

Tyagi P, Yadav SP, Singh SP (2009) Efficiency analysis of schools using DEA: a case study of Uttar Pradesh state in India. https://www.academia.edu/7539059/Efficiency_analysis_of_schools_using_DEA_A_case_study_of_Uttar_Pradesh_state_in_India

Chapter 2
An Overview of the Existing Literature and Its Linkages with the Present Book

Abstract This chapter provides an overview of the existing literature on the technical efficiency of education sector. The concept of output and input oriented measures of technical efficiency is illustrated. After describing the methodology of estimating technical efficiency using different approaches; the nonparametric data envelopment analysis (DEA, the deterministic frontier approach) and stochastic frontier production function, the chapter summarizes different studies of technical efficiency on education sector around the globe on school and higher education along with the relevant studies for the Indian economy. The connection between the existing literature on the technical efficiency of education sector and the book is highlighted.

2.1 Introduction

Although Debreu (1951), Koopmans (1951) tried to design some idea on the measurement of efficiency of a producing unit, the effective measurement of Technical Efficiency was started with the analysis of Farrell (1957). He distinguished between Technical Efficiency (TE) and Allocative Efficiency (AE). According to Farrell, in case of TE, a comparison can be made either between observed output and the maximum potential output obtainable from the given inputs (termed as '*output-oriented efficiency*') or between the observed inputs and the minimum possible inputs required to produce a given level of output (termed as '*input-oriented efficiency*'). *Input oriented* technical efficiency measure deals with the maximum amount of input quantities, which can be proportionately reduced without changing quantities produced as output. *Output oriented* technical efficiency deals with the maximum output quantities that can be proportionately increased without altering input quantities. In contrast, the AE is defined as the capability of a producing unit to combine inputs and outputs in optimal proportions, given their respective prices and production technology.[1]

Following Farrell's (1957) substantive theoretical and empirical literature, two alternative methods are observed to measure TE scores of a producing unit—(i) non

[1]Refer Battese and Coelli (1988, pp. 134–140), Lovell (1993, p. 40).

A. Ghose, *Efficiency of Elementary Education in India*,
SpringerBriefs in Economics, DOI 10.1007/978-81-322-3661-0_2

parametric Data Envelopment Analysis that involves mathematical programming procedures and (ii) Stochastic Frontier Models[2] containing parametric econometric methods. The production frontier is the locus of all maximum possible levels of output that could be produced, using the existing production technology, at all feasible combinations of quantities of various inputs. However, a producing unit, with its observed use of various inputs, may be located below this production frontier—termed as "Technically Inefficient Producing Unit" and the further away it is placed from this frontier, the larger is its extent of Technical Inefficiency.[3]

2.2 A Survey of Methodologies for Estimating Technical Efficiency and the Literature on Efficiency of Education Sector

2.2.1 The Survey of Methodologies for Estimating Technical Efficiency

A production function is the maximum possible output which can be produced from given quantities of a set of inputs. Similarly, a cost function gives the minimum level of cost at which a particular quantity of output can be produced, given input prices. The word 'frontier' may be meaningfully applied in each case because the function sets a limit to the range of possible observations. Thus there exist points below the production frontier but no point lie above it (similarly, all observations must lie on or above cost frontier). The amount by which a producing unit lies below its production frontier (or above its cost frontier) can be regarded as a measure of inefficiency. *In efficiency analysis it is not assumed that the production unit always behaves optimally and hence they can operate inefficiently. Efficiency measurement is a two stage problem—In order to judge the performance of the production units, a benchmark production function has to be constructed which is called as frontier, and is supposed to be perfectly efficient. The method of comparing the observed performance of production unit with the postulated standard of perfect efficiency is the basic problem of measuring efficiency.*

In this context a distinction needs to be drawn between Technical Efficiency (TE) and Allocative Efficiency (AE).

Let x denote the vector of n inputs that a producing unit uses to produce a single output y. Let p denote the vector of input prices, which are assumed to be positive and fixed. Then efficient transformation of inputs into output is characterized by the production function, $y = f(x)$, which shows the maximum output y obtainable from a given combination of inputs x.

---

[2]This model was independently developed by Aigner et al. (1977), Meeusen and Broeck (1977).

[3]For detail theory, refer Lovell (1993, p. 40), Coelli et al. (1998, pp. 134–140).

Let (y′, x′) be the observed production plan of the firm. This plan is said to be technically efficient if y′ = f(x′) and technically inefficient if y′ < f(x′). Clearly, from the definition of the production function y′ cannot exceed f(x′). A measure of TE is the ratio of y′ to f(x′), that must lie between 0 and 1.

The observed production plan (y′, x′) is said to be allocatively efficient if the ratio of marginal productivities of any two factors is equal to the corresponding factor price ratio

$$\text{i.e.}\ f_i(x')/f_j(x') = p_i/p_j\ \text{for all}\ i, j$$

The production plan is allocatively inefficient if this equation is invalid for some pair of inputs.

The present book deals with the measurement of TE.

Figure 2.1 shows both the *input and output oriented measures of technical efficiencies* in case of single input and output.

In Fig. 2.1 input x is measured along the horizontal axis and output y is measured along the vertical axis. Point A (x_0, y_0) represents the actual input-output bundle of a DMU, A. Now $y^* = f(x_0)$, where y* is the maximum output producible from input x_0. The *output-oriented* measure of technical efficiency of Decision Making Unit (DMU) A $= \frac{y_0}{y^*}$ which is the comparison of actual output with the maximum producible quantity from the observed input. Now for the same output bundle y_0, the input quantity can be reduced proportionately till the frontier is reached. So, y_0 can be produced from input x*. Thus the *input-oriented* technical efficiency measure for DMU A $= \frac{x^*}{x_0}$. The TE score of a DMU takes a value between 0 and 1. A value of one indicates the DMU is fully technically efficient.

Research on Efficiency Measurement has, since the seminal work of Farrell (1957) bifurcated, with economists typically following the route of Statistical

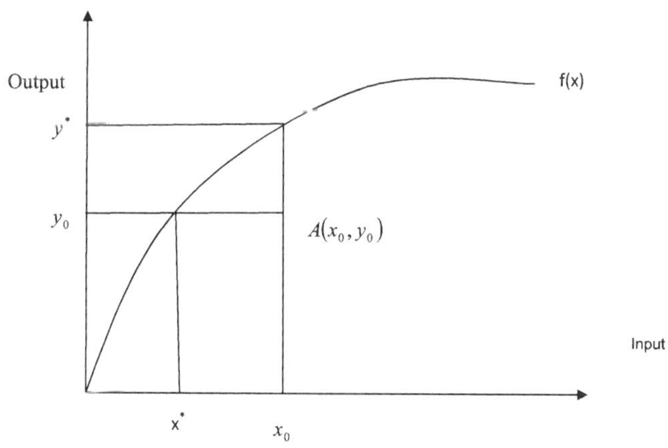

Fig. 2.1 Output and input oriented measures of technical efficiency

analysis (Aigner et al. 1977) and management scientists characteristically opting for non-parametric route grounded in linear programming (Charnes et al. (CCR) 1978). The former approach has come to be known as Stochastic Frontier analysis, the later as Data Envelopment Analysis (DEA) which is basically a linear programming method. Charnes et al. (CCR) (1978, 1981) introduced the method of DEA to address the problem of efficiency measurement for decision making units (DMU) with multiple inputs and multiple outputs in a school setting. They coined the phrase decision making units to include non-market agencies like schools, hospitals, courts which produce identifiable and measurable output from measurable inputs but generally lack market prices of outputs (and often some inputs as well). Thus, the estimation of efficiency score for primary and upper primary level of education in India with the help of DEA will certainly be an interesting issue. The advantage of DEA analysis basically is that it is not dependent on the prior specification of functional form or the criterion function.

TE of the DMU depends also on the assumption of returns to scale. Two different assumptions can be made, i.e. constant return to scale (CRS) and variable returns to scale (VRS). The CRS describes the fact that output will change by the same proportion as inputs are changed (e.g. a doubling of all inputs will double output). On the other hand, VRS reflects the fact that production technology may exhibit increasing, constant and decreasing returns to scale. If there are economies of scale, then doubling all inputs should lead to more than a doubling of output. Figure 2.2 illustrates the basic ideas behind DEA and return to scale. Four data points (A, C, B′, and D) are used here to describe the efficient frontier and the level of capacity utilization under VRS. In a simple one output case only B is inefficient, lies below the frontier, i.e. shows capacity underutilization. So unit B can produce more output at point B′ on the frontier (which is equal to theoretical maximum) utilizing same level of input at X_1. Under CRS the frontier is defined by point C for all points along the frontier, with all other points falling below the frontier (hence indicating capacity underutilization). So capacity output corresponding to VRS is smaller than the capacity output corresponding to CRS.

Fig. 2.2 The production frontier and returns to scale

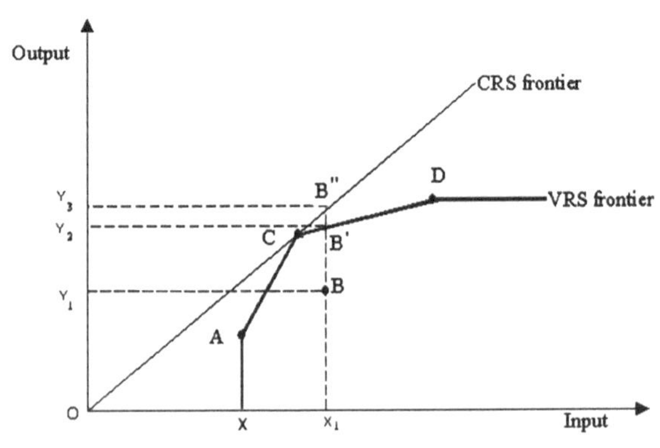

The assumption of CRS is restrictive; a more generalized case will be the assumption of VRS. *Using the actual input output bundle* and a number of fairly general assumptions about the nature of the underlying production technology, namely, (i) all actually observed input-output combinations are feasible, (ii) the production possibility set is convex, (iii) inputs are freely disposable, (iv) outputs are freely disposable, with the help of *DEA* Banker, Charnes and Cooper (BCC) (Banker et al. 1984), under VRS *derives a benchmark output quantity without any prior specification of the production frontier* applying a linear programming (LP) problem, with which the actual output of a DMU can be compared for efficiency measurement.

The present book following BCC estimates both output and input oriented measure of TE using DEA under VRS for primary and upper primary level of education of all the States and union territories in India over the period 2005–06 to 2010–11.

2.2.1.1 Estimation of Output Oriented Measure of Technical Efficiency Using DEA

It is supposed that there are N firms. Each of them is producing 'g' outputs using 'h' inputs. The firm t uses input bundle $x^t = (x_{1t,}x_{2t,\dots}x_{ht})$ and produces the output bundle $y^t = (y_{1t,}y_{2t,\dots}y_{gt})$. Technology can either follow CRS or VRS.

The production possibility set corresponding to CRS can be defined as

$$T^{CRS} = \left\{(x, y) : x \geq \sum_{j=1}^{N} \lambda_j x^t; y \leq \sum_{j=1}^{N} \lambda_j y^t; \lambda_j \geq 0; (j = 1, 2, \dots N)\right\} \tag{2.1}$$

The specific production possibility set under VRS is given by

$$T^{VRS} = \left\{(x, y) : x \geq \sum_{j=1}^{N} \lambda_j x^t; y \leq \sum_{j=1}^{N} \lambda_j y^t; \sum_{j=1}^{N} \lambda_j = 1; \lambda_j \geq 0; (j = 1, 2 \dots N)\right\} \tag{2.2}$$

The output oriented measure of TE of any firm t under *CRS technology* requires the solution of the following LP problem

$$\max \phi$$

$$\text{Subject to} \quad \sum_{j=1}^{N} \lambda_j y_{rj} \geq \phi y_{rt}; \qquad (r = 1, 2, \dots .g);$$

$$\sum_{j=1}^{N} \lambda_j x_{ij} \leq x_{it}; \, (i = 1, 2, \ldots .h);$$

$$\phi \text{ free}, \; \lambda_j \geq 0; \quad (j = 1, 2 \ldots N) \tag{2.3}$$

Output oriented TE of firm t can be determined by using Eq. (2.4).

$$TE_o^{ct} = TE_o^{ct}(x^t, y^t) = \frac{1}{\phi^*} \tag{2.4}$$

where ϕ^* is the solution of Eq. (2.3) showing the maximum value of ϕ. y* is the maximum output bundle producible from input bundle x^t and is defined as $y^* = \phi^* y^t$. Under VRS, max $\phi, \phi^{'}$, can be determined by solving Eq. (2.3) along with the constraint $\sum_{j=1}^{N} \lambda_j = 1$, taking into account the VRS frontier (Eq. (2.2)). Knowing $\phi^{'}$, TE of the firm can be solved using similar methodology corresponding to CRS.

2.2.1.2 Estimation of Input Oriented Measure of Technical Efficiency Using DEA

The input-oriented measure of technical efficiency of any firm t under CRS requires the solution of the following LP problem

$$\min \theta$$

$$\text{Subject to} \quad \sum_{j=1}^{N} \lambda_j y_{rj} \geq y_{rt;} \quad (\text{r} = 1, 2 \ldots \text{g})$$

$$\sum_{j=1}^{N} \lambda_j x_{ij} \leq \theta x_{it}; \quad (\text{i} = 1, 2 \ldots \text{h})$$

$$\theta \, \text{free}, \quad \lambda_j \geq 0, \quad (\text{j} = 1, 2 \ldots \text{N}) \tag{2.5}$$

The input-oriented technical efficiency of firm t under CRS is

$$TE_{IN}^{ct} = TE_{IN}^{ct}(x^t, y^t) = \theta^* \in T^{CRS} \tag{2.6}$$

where $\theta^* = \min \theta : (\theta x^t, y^t) \in T^{CRS}$.

Thus knowing θ^* by solving Eq. (2.5) input oriented TE of firm t can be determined by using Eq. (2.6).

The input oriented measure of TE of any firm t under VRS can be determined by solving problem (2.5) along with the constraint $\sum_{j=1}^{N} \lambda_j = 1$, considering VRS frontier.

2.2.1.3 Representation of Input Slack

In LP models radial measures of efficiency is obtained. Here efficiencies are measured along a ray from the origin to the observed production point. In such a radial projection of an observed input-output bundle onto the frontier, sometimes all the inputs used are not potentially reduced. The horizontal or vertical portion of an isoquant accounts for inefficiency in usage of inputs. As a result there may be the possibility of the existence of input slack for the case of multiple input output production process. Among the output produced by firm t, the largest output bundle with the same output mix as (y_1^t, y_2^t) that can be produced from the input bundle (x_1^*, x_2^*) is $(\phi^* y_1^*, \phi^* y_2^*)$.

It is sometimes possible to expand individual outputs by a factor larger than ϕ^*. It is also possible that firm t may not entirely use up all the individual components of the input bundle to produce the expanded output bundle. Hence all the inputs used are not potentially reduced.

The input slack variable can be defined as

$$s_i^- = x_{it} - x_{it}^*, \quad (i = 1, 2 \ldots h)$$

2.2.1.4 Representation of Underutilization of Inputs

The existence of inefficiency in input utilization basically implies existence of radial and or slack movement. The extent of underutilization of input can be measured by sum of radial and slack movement.

The input slack is explained in Fig. 2.3.

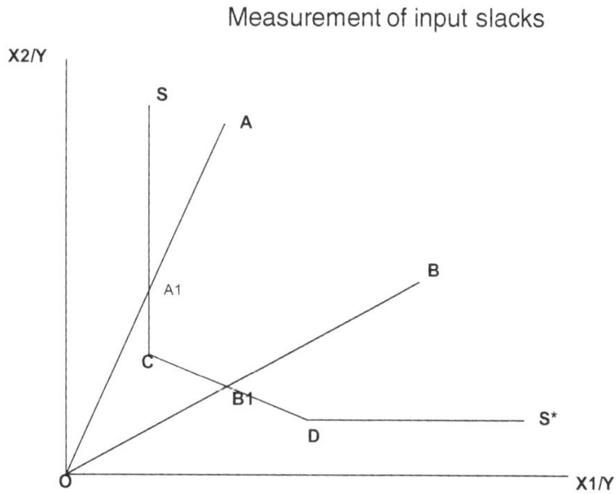

Fig. 2.3 Measurement of input slack

In the Fig. 2.3 c, d are two efficient DMU which are on the frontier. DMU A and B are inefficient. Point A_1 is on the frontier but here also the DMU is inefficient as one can reduce the amount of x_2 input by CA_1 and still produce the same output. So CA_1 is the input slack movement of input x_2 while AA_1 is the input radial movement. The underutilization of input is the sum of this radial and slack movement.

2.2.1.5 Estimation of Technical Efficiency Using Deterministic Approach

Let us consider a deterministic production frontier $f(f_i, t; \beta)$ representing the maximum producible output for the ith producing unit, under the time index t, given the non-negative input vector X_i, with the corresponding technology parameter vector β, representing technology available in the period under consideration. However, the observed output (Y_i) of that particular ith producing unit may lie below the frontier output $f(X_i, t; \beta)$ in a particular period for various reasons. For instance, the producing unit's workers may not put required effort and/or have lower ability to produce. Some owner and/or supervisor may have lower managerial capability of monitoring the effectiveness of their subordinates (Ray 2004). It can also be argued that in absence of any a priori engineering relation (that associates the combinations of inputs into their respective maximum feasible outputs), in practice, the input-output relation can only turned out to be an estimated one and hence it is quite possible that a given producing unit may not attain its maximum potentiality. This shortfall is actually attributed to the presence of technical inefficiency in that producing unit.

Given this, the production behavior of ith producing unit can be expressed as

$$Y_i = f(X_i, t; \beta)\exp(-u_i), \ldots, u_i \geq 0 \tag{2.8}$$

and a measure, termed as 'output-oriented Farrell measure' of Technical Efficiency (TE_i) of ith producing unit can be given by the ratio of the actual output to the frontier output:

$$\mathrm{TE_i} = \frac{Y_i}{f(X_i, t; \beta)} = \exp(-u_i), \ldots u_i \geq 0 \tag{2.9}$$

With $\exp(-u_i) \cong 1 - u_i$, the measure of TE ranging between 0 and 1 and varies inversely with u_i. When $u_i = 0$, $\exp(-u_i) = 1$ implying no inefficiency, so alternatively, u_i may be considered as an index of Technical Inefficiency.

The limitation of this deterministic approach is that the frontier outputs for various levels of inputs are not at all affected by any random factors like, weather, strike or by any other unforeseen factors. Aigner et al. (1977), Meeusen and Broeck (1977) independently suggested an alternative model (stochastic model) for production behavior to overcome the limitation.

2.2.1.6 Stochastic Approach

In this model an additional random error 'v' is introduced, apart from the non-negative random variable u. That particular v captures the possible unobserved random effects. This model is known as Stochastic Frontier Production Function (SFPF) model in which the frontier itself is subject to all the stochastic variations that are outside the control of the producer.

Here we have considered a stochastic production frontier of the following form:

$$Y_i = f(X_i, t; \beta)\exp(v_i) \tag{2.10}$$

This production frontier represents the maximum possible output producible with the input vector used by the ith producing unit.

β = the corresponding vector of technology parameters

v_i = a random variable seeking to capture all the random factors that are outside the control of the producer (such as, weather, strikes, factor intensity, implementation of some reform policies, natural calamities etc.). These random factors are likely to affect the production of maximum possible output. t = time period.

Actually, the ith producing unit's observed output; Y_i may lie below the frontier output due to say, the presence of workers with lower ability, poor management decisions or inadequate monitoring efforts etc. These shortfalls are captured by Technical Inefficiency of the producing unit. Since the actual output can not be higher than the frontier output, Eq. (2.10) can be modified as

$$Y_i = f(X_i, t; \beta)\exp(v_i)\exp(-u_i) \tag{2.11}$$

with $u_i \geq 0$ implying that $\exp(-u_i) \leq 1$.

So, an output-oriented Farrell measure of time-varying TE of the ith producing unit can be presented by

$$\mathrm{TE_i} = \frac{Y_i}{f(X_i, t; \beta)\exp(v_i)} = \exp(-u_i) \tag{2.12}$$

for $u_i \geq 0$ and $\mathrm{TE_i}$ varies inversely with u_i, $0 \leq TE_i \leq 1$. u_i may be taken as index of inefficiency. The output-oriented time-varying TE for ith producing unit is simply the ratio of the actual output to the frontier output.

To estimate the time-varying technical inefficiency prevailing across different firms in a particular industry, the methodology of Battese and Coelli (1993), Lundvall and Battese (2000) can be followed. From Eq. (2.12), it can be noted that v_i and u_i—two error terms are included in the expression. v_i is the usual error term of the model and is independently, identically, normally distributed with mean = 0 and variance = σ^2. u_i measures the magnitude of technical inefficiency in production prevailing in the ith producing unit. It is independently distributed from a normal distribution with mean = μ_i and variance = σ_u^2, truncated at zero. Further it is assumed that there is no correlation between v_i and u_i.

After getting different TE scores of different producing units, one may be naturally interested to stagger on the factors responsible behind the variations in TE scores. To find out the determinants of TEs, some empirical studies have suggested a two-stage procedure. In the first stage, firm-specific TE scores are estimated applying stochastic frontier production functions and in the second stage, the estimated TEs scores are regressed on a number of firm-specific variables like, firm size, capital intensity, trade-related factors etc. It is supposed that these factors might be responsible for the variations in TEs across producing units. In many cases, this two-stage procedure have yielded satisfactory results but it has long been argued that this procedure suffers from an inconsistency problem, originated from the assumption of constant $\exp(u_i)$ in the first stage, which may contradict the assumption in the second stage that the predicted efficiencies vary with the firm-specific explanatory variables (Coelli et al. 1998, pp. 207–209; Kumbhakar and Lovell 2000, pp. 262–264).

An alternative approach, developed by Battese and Coelli (1993), can be followed in which the estimation of TE scores and the explanation behind the variations in TE are done simultaneously in a single stage. In our empirical study, we have followed this single-stage procedure.

In this model, u_is are not assumed to follow an identical distribution, rather different u_is should have different means i.e., for each u_i the corresponding mean, before truncation, can be denoted by μ_i, $\forall i = 1(1)n$. So the assumption regarding the variable u_i is now modified as the following: u_is are independently distributed with same variance σ_u^2, but the mean of each u_i is different to each other: $u_i \sim idN^+(\mu_i, \sigma_u^2)$. The present model is now specified with such a stochastic frontier model in which the inefficiency effects are included as an explicit function of some firm-specific factors/variables and their associated parameters. The SFPF along with the inefficiency effects is estimated through a single-stage Maximum Likelihood Estimation (MLE) method.

The mean Technical Inefficiency is represented by

$$\mu_i = \delta' Z_i \tag{2.13}$$

and adding the relation with Eq. (2.11) we get the model for our empirical study. In Eq. (2.13), μ_i = mean before truncation for the variable u_i.

Z_i = ith producing unit's specific vector that may include exogenous and endogenous variables in explaining the inefficiency effect.

δ = associated parameters to be estimated and δ' is the transpose of δ.

It can be noted here that this assumption is consistent with the assumption that the u_i is a non-negative truncation of $N(\delta' Z_i, \sigma_u^2)$. Furthermore, u_i is specified in such a manner that we can easily obtain the density function of u_i conditional on $\varepsilon_i = v_i - u_i$ as well as the expected value of TE_i, given ε_i.[4] There may be some literature in which some alternative models are also presented for this purpose but it can be

[4]According to Battese and Coelli (1988, 1993), the expected value of TEi, given ε_i is $E[\exp(-u_i)|\varepsilon_i$.

noticed here that those models are obtained as particular cases of the models following the Eqs. (2.11) and (2.13). For example, according to Huang and Lin (1994), a non-neutral model can be built if some of the input variables of the model also appear in Z_i. Again, if Z_i vector's first element is unity with non-zero parameter associated with it, while rest of the δ s are zero, we can get the general truncated normal distribution for the u_i (proposed by Stevenson 1980; Battese et al. 1988). If elements of δ is a null vector, the half-normal distribution for the u_is are obtained. It is to be noted here that Y_i should not be included in the Z_i vector; Z_i may be defined in terms of the level of an input, but not output

2.2.2 *Estimation of Technical Efficiency Score for Education Sector*

TE scores is estimated mainly by applying non-parametric Data Envelopment Analysis (DEA) which basically rests on assumed production relationship between input and outputs. *In the literature, estimation of efficiency of a school is* basically rests on assumed production relationship between input and outputs. Following Ray (2004) educational production function can be defined as:

$$Y = A\ (X1\ldots Xm,),$$

where Y is some measure of school output—for example, enrolment ratio and or marks obtained in standardized examination system.

X1,…Xm are the variables measuring the school environment. The variables here would typically include the amount and quality of teaching services, the physical infrastructure or facilities of the school.

The term A can be thought of as a shift parameter, being a function of (i) I_1,…In, the variables representing favourable Infrastructure facilities that promote TE level, (ii) PR_1,…PRq, the variables representing the poor infrastructure facilities that can reduce TE level, (i) Zn,…Zp the variables representing environmental influences on learning outside the school—These variables take care of the general environment of learning that the students faces.

Educational achievement can be viewed as a production process, where inputs of resources are applied to the relatively "unfinished" child, and an output-pupil achievement results. The objective is to generate the maximum achievement using a given amount of school resources. Some studies also uses Stochastic Production Frontier Model.

2.2.2.1 International Literature Relating to Studies on Technical Efficiency of Education Sector

A number studies are available dealing with estimation of TE score of the school and higher education, Universities and Research Institutes and also for Further Education around the globe.

International Literature Relating to Studies on Technical Efficiency of Schools

Mancebon and Eduardo (1999) evaluated the efficiency of a sample of Spanish secondary schools, paying particular attention to the theoretical specification of the measurement model. They tried to demonstrate that, in order for a study of this nature to have the minimum solvency, it is the special characteristics of the education production process that must form the basic guidelines to be followed by researchers. They also highlighted the characteristics that differentiate the most efficient schools from the least efficient, and emphasized the importance of completing the information supplied by the quantitative methods of educational evaluation (such as data envelopment analysis), with the data of qualitative nature obtained by way of surveys directed at the pupils (customers) and the school decision-makers.

Chakraborty et al. (2001) uses both the stochastic and nonstochastic production function approach to measure technical efficiency in public education in Utah. The stochastic specification estimates technical efficiency assuming half normal and exponential distributions. The nonstochastic specification uses two stage data envelopment analysis (DEA) to separate the effects of fixed inputs on the measure of technical efficiency. The empirical analysis shows substantial variation in efficiency among school districts. Although these measures are incentive to the specific distributional assumptions about the one-sided component of the error term in the stochastic specification, they are sensitive to the treatment of fixed socio-economic inputs in the two-stage DEA.

Lassibille and Tan (2001) examined whether explosive growth of private secondary schools in Tanzania led to efficient operations in terms of student learning by comparing the efficiency of four types of schools that make up the majority of schools in the country: Government and Community schools in the public sector, and Christian and Wazazi schools in the private sector. Using longitudinal data from a 1994 retrospective survey of students in some 150 schools, they estimated separate achievement models for these four school types, with corrections for possible selection bias in school choice, and then used the results to simulate performance gaps across them. The simulations indicate that both types of private schools are less efficient than both types of public schools in the sense that, on average, a student with a given set of personal and family characteristics would do better in either type of public school than in either type of private school, after netting out differences in the endowment of school resources across school types. In the public sector, they found that Community schools are more efficient that Government schools. Based on their study they suggested the need for a strong and productive private sector, and recommend the creation of networking opportunities for private school managers to exchange experiences with their public-school counterparts, and the creation of mechanisms for private schools to compete for public funding to support their operations.

Mizala et al. (2002) assesses the technical efficiency of schools in Chile, which is defined as the capacity of schools to generate the maximum output (academic achievement) given the quantity of inputs they use. Two alternative methodological approaches for measuring efficiency are used stochastic production frontier and DEA. Each of these techniques has advantages and limitations, which are discussed in the paper; they lead, however, to the same conclusions when a sample of 2000 schools is analyzed. The results obtained provide interesting points for educational policy discussion in Chile.

Barbetta and Turati (2003) dealt with the role of proprietary structure in explaining efficiency within the Italian school industry taking a sample of 497 schools located in Piemonte, a region in the North-Western part of the country and distinguishing between public, private for-profit and private nonprofit schools. In stage one of the analyses, they provide robust estimates of efficiency scores, using the two most widely known techniques in applied works, namely DEA and Stochastic Frontiers. In stage two, they suggested that proprietary structure matters in explaining efficiency. Nonprofit schools are more efficient than public ones, whereas for-profit counterparts are outperformed by public producers. Moreover, it was that foreign and disabled students affect negatively efficiency, raising concerns for cream-skimming practices among private producers. Finally, school size is another important determinant of efficiency.

Oliveira and Santos (2005) used Free Disposal Hull (FDH) reference technology that contains information both on inputs and outputs to determine radial technical efficiency scores and slacks for a sample of Portuguese secondary schools. This is the study using FDH at the school level, effectively relaxing the convexity assumption. A two-stage approach is used, whereby the significant environmental variables that explain FDH efficiency scores and slacks are identified. For the purpose of statistical inference, the first application of the bootstrapping algorithms suggested by Simar and Wilson (2004) is conducted. The study concludes that the unemployment rate, access to health care services, adult education and living infrastructures are determinants of school efficiency. The differences between the coast and the interior of Portugal seem to be more relevant, as far as school efficiency is concerned, than whether or not the school belongs to one of the major coast metropolitan areas.

Borge and Naper (2005) performs an efficiency analysis of the lower secondary school sector in Norway. The efficiency potential is calculated to 14 % based on a DEA analysis with grades in core subjects (adjusted for student characteristics and family background) as outputs. The analysis of the determinants of efficiency indicates that a high level of municipal revenue, a high degree of party fragmentation, and a high share of socialists in the local council are associated with low educational efficiency. The negative effects of the share of socialists and party fragmentation seem to reflect both higher resource use and lower student performance.

Grosskopf et al. (2014) compares TE of charter school primary and secondary campuses with that of comparable campuses in traditional Texas school districts. Charter schools are hybrids—publicly funded, but not required to meet all the state regulations relevant for traditional schools. Student performance is measured using value added on standardized tests in reading and mathematics, and efficiency is measured using the input distance function. The analysis suggests that at least in Texas, charter schools are substantially more efficient than traditional public schools.

Naper (2010) analyzed the relationship between teacher hiring practices and educational efficiency in Norwegian school districts. The hiring decision is made at the school level by the principal or at the school district level. According to the data, efficiency is the highest in districts where hiring is decentralized. Hiring practices are decided by the school district, and linear estimates of the effect of decentralized hiring on efficiency may be biased because of non-random selection. First, he approaches this problem by including a large set of controls in a school district level analysis, which does not alter the qualitative result. Second, he performs a school level analysis with district fixed effects. The results indicate, as expected, that the effect of decentralization is stronger for schools facing excess teacher supply than for schools without excess supply.

Alexander et al. (2010) conducted a two-stage (DEA and regression) analysis of the efficiency of New Zealand secondary schools. Unlike previous applications of two-stage semi parametric modeling of the school "production process", they use Simar and Wilson's double bootstrap procedure, which permits valid inference in the presence of unknown serial correlation in the efficiency scores. They are therefore able to draw robust conclusions about a system that has undergone extensive reforms with respect to ideas high on the educational agenda such as decentralized school management and parental choice. Most importantly, they find that school type affects school efficiency and so too does teacher quality.

Burney et al. (2010) examined the efficiency of public schools in Kuwait over each school level (kindergarten, primary, intermediate, and secondary) and six academic years (1979/80, 1984/85, 1989/90, 1994/95, 1999/2000 and 2004/05). The analysis is based on the entire public school population in the country and relies on a two-stage approach. In the first stage, estimates of technical, scale, allocative, and economic efficiencies are obtained on the basis of DEA technique. The second stage relates to finding out determinants of TE using school characteristics employing the Tobit regression model. The explanatory variables included in the regression model are the schools' regional location, teachers' salary, proportion of teaching staff that are Kuwaitis, and whether a school is all-boys' or all-girls'. The estimates show that the public schools in Kuwait use more resources for the level of school output, operate below the optimum size (returns to scale are generally increasing), and use non-optimal input proportions. Teachers' salary is found to have positive effect on technical efficiency while the proportion of Kuwaiti teaching staff has a negative impact. All-girls schools are found to have higher efficiency than all-boys schools.

Cherchye et al. (2010) presented a nonparametric approach for efficiency and equity evaluation in education using a nonparametric DEA. The model accounts for the fact that typically minimal prior structure is available for the behavior (objectives and feasibility set) under evaluation. It allows for uncertainty in the data, while it corrects for exogenous 'environmental' characteristics that are specific to each pupil. They propose two multidimensional stochastic dominance criteria as naturally complementary aggregation criteria for comparing the performance of different school types (private and public schools). While the first criterion only accounts for efficiency, the second criterion also take equity into consideration. The model is applied for comparing private (but publicly funded) and public primary schools in Flanders. The application finds that no school type robustly dominates another type when controlling for the school environment and taking equity into account. More generally, it demonstrates the usefulness of the nonparametric approach, which includes environmental and equity considerations, for obtaining 'fair' performance comparisons in the public sector context.

Kirjavainen (2012) used different stochastic frontier models for panel data to estimate education production functions and the efficiency of Finnish general upper secondary schools. Grades in the matriculation examination are used as an output and explained with the comprehensive school grade point average, parental socioeconomic background, school resources, the length of studies and the decentralization of test-taking. Heterogeneity across schools is allowed for by estimating true random effect (TRE), random parameter (RP) and true fixed effect (TFE) models. The results show that inefficiency and rankings of schools based on their inefficiency scores vary considerably depending on the type of stochastic frontier model applied. The lowest estimates for inefficiency are obtained with TRE, RP and TFE models, which separate time-constant random or fixed effects from inefficiency. The length of studies and the decentralization of test-taking negatively affect student achievement.

Aristovnik (2013) measured relative efficiency in utilizing public education expenditures in the new EU member states in comparison to the selected EU (plus Croatia) and OECD countries. As resources allocated to education are significantly limited, a special emphasis should be given to their efficient use regarding the institutional and legal constraints. An analysis of (output-oriented) efficiency measures by using DEA shows that among the new EU member states Hungary, Estonia and Slovenia seem to be good benchmark countries in the field of primary, secondary and tertiary education, respectively. The empirical results also suggest that, in general, new EU member states show relatively high efficiency in tertiary education efficiency measures.

Agasisti (2013) using DEA computed efficiency scores for a sample of Italian schools by employing OECD-PISA2006 data aggregated at school level. Different versions of the DEA models were estimated to test result robustness, including a DEA bootstrapping procedure. In a second-stage analysis, the factors affecting school efficiency are investigated through a Tobit regression. Among these factors, alternative indicators of competition were included. The results show that at least one indicator of competition is statistically associated with higher performances of schools, suggesting that there is a potential role for improving school results by increasing the number of schools competing each other.

Cuellar and Felipe (2014) appraised quantitatively the efficiency of public expenditure of 15 Latin American countries using cross-country data for averages between 2000 and 2009. For this purpose two non-parametric methods are used: DEA and Free Disposal Hull (FDH). Selected output indicators in primary and secondary school are evaluated respect to public spending in education per student. As a study case, Colombia's efficiency scores are compared with the most efficient peers in each of the educational levels to identify best practices and achieve better results.

Blackburn et al. (2014) applied a public sector DEA model to estimate the efficiency of Australian primary and secondary schools. Standard microeconomic production theory showing the transformation of inputs into outputs is extended to allow nondiscretionary environmental variables characteristic of educational production. Failure to properly control for the socioeconomic environment leads to inappropriate comparisons and biased efficiency estimates. They employ a conditional estimator that does not allow a school with a better environment to serve as a benchmark for a school with a worse environment. The results suggest that Australian schools are moderately inefficient and that efficiency increases for the quintile of schools with the most favorable environment. Further, efficiency gains are realized with increasing enrollment.

Bogetoftet al. (2015) focusing in particular on upper secondary education examined whether the relatively high level of expenditure on education in the Nordic countries is matched by high output from the educational sector, both in terms of student enrolment and indicators of output quality in the form of graduation/completion rates and expected earnings after completed education. The paper uses DEA to compare (benchmark) the Nordic countries with a relevant group of rich OECD countries and calculate input efficiency scores for each country. The paper estimates a wide range of specifications in order to analyze different aspects of efficiency. In purely quantitative models (where inputs and outputs are expenditure and number of students at different levels of the educational system) and in models where graduation or completion rates are included as indicators of output quality, Finland is the most efficient Nordic country (often fully efficient), whereas Sweden and especially Norway and Denmark are clearly inefficient. However, using PISA test scores as indicators of student input quality in upper secondary education reduces the inefficiencies of these three countries. Also, when expected earnings after completed education are used as an indicator of output quality, all Nordic countries are estimated to be fully efficient (or nearly so).

International Literature Relating to Studies on Technical Efficiency of Higher and Further Education

Ng and Li (2000) utilizing data from 84 key chinese higher education institutions attempted to examine the effectiveness of the Education Reform implemented in the mid-1980s in China. With focus on the research performance of the institutions, individual institution efficiency is computed by the method of data envelopment analysis. Regional differences in the efficiency of the institutions are also addressed. It is found that research performance of institutions across regions has improved, although the institutions as a whole have remained inefficient 1993–1995. Institutions located in the East region turn out to have out-performed those in the Central and the West regions. In addition, the decomposition of the group efficiency measure indicates that, for the 3 years under study, the 84 key institutions suffered from technical, allocative and reallocative inefficiency.

Abbott and Doucouliagos (2002) used Data Envelopment Analysis to derive estimates of the technical and scale efficiency of Victorian Technical and Further Education Institutes in 1995. The results reveal substantial dispersion in technical and scale efficiencies. Regression analysis is used to identify variables which are associated with technical inefficiency.

Flegg et al. (2004) applied DEA to examine the technical efficiency (TE) of 45 British universities in the period 1980/81–1992/93. This period was chosen primarily because it was characterized by major changes in public funding and in student: staff ratios. To shed light on the causes of variations in efficiency, TE is decomposed into pure technical efficiency, congestion efficiency and scale efficiency. The analysis indicates that there was a substantial rise in the weighted geometric mean TE score during the study period, although this rise was most noticeable between 1987/88 and 1990/91. The rising TE scores are attributed largely to the gains in pure technical efficiency and congestion efficiency, with scale efficiency playing a minor role. The Malmquist approach is then used to distinguish between changes in TE and inter temporal shifts in the efficiency frontier. The results reveal that total factor productivity rose by 51.5 % between 1980/81 and 1992/93, and that most of this increase was due to a substantial outward shift in the efficiency frontier during this period.

Ferrari and Laureti (2005) modeled the human capital formation in the Italian university and utilizes a measure of TE to estimate the output-efficiency of human capital formation in the University of Florence, by using DEA on a selected set of inputs and outputs. It uses the Program Evaluation procedure as well, in an attempt to attribute shares of the variation in efficiency to factors that are beyond the control and factors that are under the control of the graduates and faculties.

Johnes (2006a) applied DEA and multilevel modeling to a data set of 54,564 graduates from UK universities in 1993 to assess whether the choice of technique affects the measurement of universities' performance. A methodology developed by Thanassoulis and Portela (2002; Education Economics, 10(2), pp. 183–207) allows each individual's DEA efficiency score to be decomposed into two components: one attributable to the university at which the student studied and the other attributable to the individual student. From the former component, a measure of each institution's teaching efficiency is derived and compared to the university effects from various multilevel models. The comparisons are made within four broad subjects: pure science, applied science, social science and arts. The results show that the rankings of universities derived from the DEA efficiencies which measure the universities' own performance (i.e., having excluded the efforts of the individuals) are not strongly correlated with the university rankings derived from the university effects of the multilevel models. The data were also used to perform a university-level DEA. The university efficiency scores derived from these DEAs are largely unrelated to the scores.

McMillan and Chan (2006) determined efficiency scores for Canadian universities using both DEA and stochastic frontier methods for selected specifications. The outcomes are compared. There is considerable divergence in the efficiency scores and their rankings among methods and specifications. An analysis of rankings, however, reveals that the relative positions of individual universities across sets of several efficiency rankings (e.g., all the data envelopment analysis and stochastic frontier outcomes) demonstrate an underlying consistency.

High-efficiency and low-efficiency groups are evidenced but the rank for most universities is not significantly different from that of many others. The results emphasize the need for caution when employing efficiency scores for management and policy purposes, and they recommend looking for confirmation across viable alternatives.

Johnes (2006b) examined efficiency in the context of higher education with an application of DEA to a data set of more than 100 Higher Education Institute (HEIs) in England using data for the year 2000/01. Technical and scale efficiency in the English higher education sector appear to be high on average. The Pastor, Ruiz and Sirvent (2002). Test for comparing nested DEA models is useful in reducing the full model to a smaller 'significant' set of inputs and outputs. Thus, the quantity and quality of undergraduates, the quantity of postgraduates, expenditure on administration, and the value of interest payments and depreciation are significant inputs to, and the quantity and quality of undergraduate degrees, the quantity of postgraduate degrees and research are significant outputs in the English higher education production process. The possibility of differences in the production frontier (and hence the distribution of efficiencies) of three distinct groups of HEIs is explored using a test proposed by Charnes et al. (1981. Management Science, 27(6), 668–697) but no significant differences are found. Bootstrapping procedures, however, suggest that differences between the most and least efficient English HEIs are significant.

Fernando and Emilyn (2007) estimated relative efficiency and productive performance of 13 colleges at the University of Santo Tomas (UST), using data envelopment analysis (DEA)—Malmquist indices and a multi-stage model. Total factor productivity (TFP) is measured for a sample of 13 colleges at UST over the period 1998–2003. Empirical results show that the main contributing factor to TFP growth is efficiency change. That is, UST colleges are technically operating efficiently in the frontier technology; though there is a downward shift in the technological advancement. The results further imply that with the use of output–input mix, UST colleges as a whole have recorded a higher level of technical efficiency than innovation. These new findings contribute significantly to the existing literature on efficiency and productive performance in the education sector.

Johnes (2008) used a distance function approach to derive Malmquist productivity indexes for 112 English higher education institutions (HEIs) over the period 1996/97 to 2004/5. The analysis shows that HEIs have experienced an annual average increase in productivity of 1 %. Further investigation reveals that HEIs have enjoyed an annual average increase in technology of 6 % combined with a decrease in TE of 5 %. Rapid changes in the higher education sector appear to have had a positive effect on the technology of production but this has been achieved at the cost of lower technical efficiency.

Agasisti and Johnes (2009) employed DEA to compute TE of Italian and English higher education institutions. The results show that, in relation to the country-specific frontier, institutions in both countries are typically very efficient. However, institutions in England are more efficient than those in Italy when we compare jointly their performances. They also look at the evolution of technical efficiency scores over a four-year period, and find that, in line with an error-correction hypothesis, Italian universities are improving their technical efficiency while English universities are obtaining stable scores. Policy implications are also addressed.

Agasisti and Bianco (2009) analyzed the effects of teaching reforms in Italy by estimating TE of higher education using DEA. These were introduced in 1999, and changed the entire organization of university courses, where the Bachelor-Master (BA-MA) structure was adopted. The changes introduced by the reforms are modeled within the adopted framework: the effects of teaching reforms are investigated as determinants of efficiency improvements. Malmquist index analysis, suggest that efficiency of the higher education sector as a whole improved in the period 1998/1999 to 2003/2004. Despite the fact that teaching reforms led to worse performance in the first year, in the following years productivity improved more rapidly than before.

Abbott and Doucouliagos (2009) explored the efficiency of Australian and New Zealand public universities in order to investigate the impact of competition for students from overseas on efficiency. Output distance functions are estimated using panel data for the period 1995–2002 for Australia and 1997–2003 for New Zealand. The results show that competition for overseas students has led to increased efficiency in Australian universities. However, competition for overseas students appears to have had no effect on efficiency in New Zealand.

Bradley et al. (2010) used data for nearly 200 further education providers in England to investigate the level of efficiency and change in productivity over the period 1999–2003. Using data envelopment analysis they found that the mean provider efficiency varies between 83 and 90 % over the period. Productivity change over the period was around 12 %, and this comprised 8 % technology change and 4 % technical efficiency change. A multivariate analysis is therefore performed, which shows that, in general, student-related variables such as gender, ethnic and age mix are more important than staff-related variables in determining efficiency levels. The local unemployment rate also has an effect on provider efficiency. The policy implications of the results are that further education providers should implement strategies to improve the completion and achievement rates of white males, and should also offer increased administrative support to teachers.

Given the fact that due to tight public budget constraints, the efficiency of publicly financed universities in Germany is receiving increasing attention in the academic as well as in the public discourse, Pohl and Kempkes (2010) analyzed the efficiency of 72 public German universities for the years 1998–2003, applying DEA and stochastic frontier analysis. Contrary to earlier studies, they account for the faculty composition of universities which proves to be an essential element in the efficiency of higher education. Their main finding is that East German universities have performed better in total factor productivity change compared to those in West Germany. However, when looking at mean efficiency scores over the sample period, West German universities still appear at the top end of relative efficiency outcomes.

Johnes et al. (2010) investigates efficiency levels by subject of study within further education (FE) colleges. Mean overall technical efficiency is found to vary from 75 to 86 % in the worst- and best-performing subject areas, respectively.

Statistical analysis of efficiency reveals that, while student and teacher composition and regional characteristics affect efficiency in each subject, the strength of these effects can vary by subject. This has the clear policy implication that strategies to improve efficiency in English FE must be devised and operated at subject rather than provider level.

Since in a context of financial stringency like that characterizing the current economic landscape in Portugal and in several other countries, accountability and efficiency questions gain an additional relevance in the higher education sector, Cunha and Rocha (2012) applied DEA techniques to evaluate the comparative efficiency of public higher education institutions in Portugal. The analysis is performed for three separate groups: public universities, public polytechnics and the several faculties of University of Porto. The results suggest that a great portion of institutions may be working inefficiently, contributing to a significant waste of resources.

Foltz et al. (2012) investigated the determinants of TE and technological progress at US research universities. It relies on a unique panel data set of multiple outputs and inputs from 92 universities covering the period 1981–1998. Over that time span, US universities experienced large increases in industry funding and in academic patenting activity. In this context, the directional distance function and a nonparametric representation of the underlying production technology are combined to obtain estimates of productivity growth and TE. An econometric analysis is then presented to examine the determinants of TE and the rate of technological progress. The results show how changes in funding sources for US research universities affects research performance.

Wolszczak-Derlac (2014) used DEA to evaluate the relative efficiency of 500 higher education institutions (HEIs) in ten European countries and the U.S. for the period between 2000 and 2010. Efficiency scores are determined using different input-output sets (inputs: total revenue, academic staff, administration staff, total number of students; outputs: total number of publications, number of scientific articles, graduates) and considering different frontiers: global frontiers (all HEIs pooled together) and a regional frontier (Europe and the U.S. having their own frontiers). Changes in total factor productivity are assessed by means of the Malmquist index and are decomposed into pure efficiency changes and frontier shifts. Also investigated are the external factors affecting the degree of HEI inefficiency, e.g. institutional settings (size and department composition), location, funding structure (using two-stage DEA analysis following the bootstrap procedure proposed by Simar and Wilson 2007). Specifically, it is found that the role of the university funding structure in HEI technical efficiency is different in Europe and in the U.S. Increased government funding is associated with an increase in inefficiency only in the case of European units, while the share of funds from tuition fees decreases the efficiency of American public institutions but relates to efficiency improvements in European universities.

Jonhes (2014) explored the issue of efficiency in English higher education using DEA and stochastic frontier analysis to estimate an output distance function (which incorporates measures of both quantity and quality of teaching and research inputs and outputs) over a 13-year period. The study compares the efficiency estimates derived from various estimation methods, and uses the results to provide guidance to researchers, managers and policymakers on undertaking efficiency studies. The length of the study under consideration allows a preliminary statistical investigation of the effects on efficiency of merger activity in higher education.

Barra and Zotti (2016) applied data envelopment analysis (DEA) to assess technical efficiency in a big public university. Particular attention has been paid to two main activities, teaching and research, and on two large groups, the Science and Technology (ST) sector and the Humanity and Social Science (HSS) sector. The findings, based to data from 2005 to 2009, suggest that the ST sector is more efficient in terms of quality of research than the HSS sector that instead achieves higher efficiency in teaching activities. A bootstrap technique is also used to provide confidence intervals for efficiency scores and to obtain bias-corrected estimates. The Malmquist index is calculated to measure changes in productivity.

Technical Efficiency Analysis for the Indian Education Sector

Kingdon (1996) presented empirical evidence on the relative quality and efficiency of private and government-funded schools in urban India, using data from Uttar Pradesh. The results suggest that standardizing for home background and controlling for sample selectivity greatly reduces the raw average achievement advantage of private school students over public school students, but does not wipe it out. Private schools' standardized achievement advantage (or better quality) is complemented by their lower unit costs to enable them to be more efficient. The results support much of the existing evidence on the relative efficiency of private and public schools.

Tyagi (2009) assessed the technical efficiency and efficiency differences among 348 elementary schools of Uttar Pradesh state in India by using DEA.

Sankar (2007) considered efficiency of *elementary education as a whole* for different states of India considering two points of time: the mid-1990s and 2004–05 but not for primary and upper primary level of education separately. In Sankar (2007) the factors that contribute to the "efficiency scores" largely remain unexplained—However, some of the regressions showed the role of density of population, a proxy to look at concentration factor and hence the scope for economies of scales to operate, as significant.

Sengupta and Pal (2010) explained the efficiency *primary education sector in India* using DISE statistics only for the year 2005–06. They identified some basic aspects of education: deprivation aspects, social aspects, policy aspects. The country has been divided into five zones: Northern, North-eastern, Eastern, Western and Southern districts respectively. Using Anand and Sen (1997) formula of Human Poverty Index (HPI) they derived Grand Poverty Index comprising of various poverty indicators of education system in India and tried to relate these with the efficiency score in DEA. The result of their study indicates that poverty indicators have negative impacts on efficiency, whereas social and policy indicators are not significantly related to the efficiency improvement.

Sengupta and Pal (2012) explained the efficiency of only primary education sector of Burdwan District of West Bengal, corresponding to a single year 2006.

Purohit (2015). Rajasthan being India's largest state comprising 10.4 % of India's total area is located on the western side of the country. The state is divided into 33 districts. Over the 1990s and early 2000s, enrolment rates at the primary level were rising and gender gap converging, though female enrolment rate is still to catch up with that of male. There also exist considerable differential across districts in the State. As per survey in 2012, overall literacy varies from 55.58 % (Jalore) to 77.48 % (in Kota). In this paper, considering the district level variations in literacy and other pertinent socio-economic variables he explores whether efficiency in education in district level enrolments is merely a reflection of the other conditions or is it owing to lack of efficient utilization of available educational input variables. Thus he estimates district level efficiency in enrolments at primary and upper-primary levels, in government and private schools, in Rajasthan and look into reasons for their differentials. Using data for the period 2008–2012 and applying stochastic frontier analysis their results indicate that a strong role is being played by economic development parameters like income and urbanization. And simultaneously direct educational interventions seem to play a positive role in enhancing enrolments at different levels. Therefore an education policy should capture district specific gaps to strengthen the outcomes. This may thus necessitate more information at district level both in terms of educational and economic parameters and this information gap needs to be overcome through planning process.

2.3 Connections of Present Book with Existing Literature

The perusal of the literature suggests the following gaps in the existing literature relating to the efficiency of elementary education sector in India. The present book attempts to overcome these above limitations and contributes to the literature in the following directions.

First of all, in contrast to existing studies the book does not assume a common frontier for all the Indian states and the union territories. As explained in Chap. 1 it is difficult to assume a common frontier for all the states and union territories in India as not all of them operate under same economic and fiscal condition. Rather, the book constructs two group frontiers: (i) for states only with GCS and (ii) for the states under SCS and UT. The book carries out the group frontier and Meta frontier analysis. The Meta frontier defines the frontier corresponding to all the 35 states and union territories taken together. In particular, Technology Closeness Ratio (TCR) measuring whether the maximum output producible from an input bundle by a school within a group is *as high as* what could be produced if the school could choose to locate anywhere in India is computed. TCR shows the divergence of the group frontiers from the Meta frontiers, to what extent group frontiers are close to the Meta frontiers. Such a computation of TCR will help us to identify whether maximum output producible by SCS is higher or lower than that could be produced under GCS, given the resources.

Secondly, the book estimates technical efficiency score of both primary and upper primary level of education for the above two groups and compares the performance of efficiency score of primary and secondary level of education for six successive years from 2005–06 to 2010–11. *While estimating technical efficiency score it takes into account both quantities as well as quality aspects of outputs and inputs. The earlier Indian studies dealing with interstate variation of technical efficiency score did not consider the quality aspects.*

Thirdly, the book measures the extent of underutilization of different inputs, for different States and union territories of India, both for primary and upper primary level of education, *the estimates of which are still lacking in the literature.*

Finally, while finding out the determinants of efficiency, it intends to take into account (i) some factors from poor infrastructure to see whether poor infrastructure inhibit the achievement of TE, (ii) some factors from favorable infrastructure to see whether favorable infrastructure induces the achievement of TE, (iii) some social indicators to investigate whether inclusion of the backward classes into the education system increases TE, (iv) some policy variables to test whether provision of more public facilities increases TE and also (v) some state level macro aggregates like per-capita net State domestic product, income inequality, and number of persons lying below the poverty line to see to what extent the general environment of the state matters in explaining TE. Also, rather than using a composite index the present book attempts to find out the individual effect of the different explanatory variables. The earlier result that social and policy indicators are not significantly related to the efficiency improvement may be due to the use of composite index. It is quite possible that some of the individual factors comprising of the composite variables are significant while the others are not. Separate regression is carried out for primary and upper primary level. *The relative sensitivity of the central-grant in explaining the efficiency performance of primary and upper-primary education of both GCS and SCS&U is estimated, which can be used for judging the efficacy of central grant in promoting technical efficiency of these two groups and there is paucity of such estimation.*

References

Abbott M, Doucouliagos H (2002) A data envelopment analysis of the efficiency of Victorian TAFE institutes. Australian Econ Rev 35(1):55–69

Abbott M, Doucouliagos C (2009) Competition and efficiency: overseas students and technical efficiency in Australian and New Zealand universities. Educ Econ 17(1):31–57

Agasisti T (2013) The efficiency of Italian secondary schools and the potential role of competition: a data envelopment analysis using OECD-PISA 2006 data. Educ Econ 21(5):520–544

Agasisti T, Bianco AD (2009) Reforming the university sector: effects on teaching efficiency-evidence from Italy. High Educ 57(4):477–498

Agasisti T, Johnes G (2009) Beyond frontiers: comparing the efficiency of higher education decision-making units across more than one country. Educ Econ 17(1):59–79

Aigner DJ, Lovell CAK, Schmidt PJ (1977) Formulation and estimation of stochastic frontier production function models. J Econ 6(1):21–37

Alexander W, Haung A, Jaforullah M (2010) A two-stage double-bootstrap data envelopment analysis of efficiency differences of New Zealand secondary schools. J Prod Anal 34(2):99–110

Anand S, Sen A (1997) Concepts of human development and poverty: a multidimensional perspective. In: Poverty and human development: human development papers 1997, pp. 1–20. United Nations Development Programme, New York

Aristovnik A (2013) Relative efficiency of education expenditures in Eastern Europe: a non-parametric approach. J Knowl Manag Econ Inf Technol 3(3):1–13

Banker RD, Charnes A, Cooper WW (1984) Some models for estimating technical and scale efficiencies in data envelopment analysis. Manag Sci 30(9):1078–1092

Barbetta GP, Turati G (2003) Efficiency of junior high schools and the role of proprietary structure. Ann Public Cooper Econ 74(4):529–551

Bradley S, Johnes J, Little A (2010) Measurement and determinants of efficiency and productivity in future education sector in England. Bull Econ Res 62(1):1–30

Barra C, Zotti R (2016) Measuring efficiency in higher education: an empirical study using a bootstrapped data envelopment analysis. Int Adv Econ Res 22(1):11–33

Battese GE, Coelli TJ (1988) Prediction of firm-level technical efficiencies with a generalized frontier production function and panel data. J Econ 38(3):387–399

Battese GE, Coelli TJ (1993) A stochastic production function incorporating a model for technical efficiency effects. Working paper no 69, Department of Econometrics, University of New England, Australia

Blackburn V, Bernman S, Ruggiero J (2014) Measuring efficiency in Australian schools: a preliminary analysis. Socio-Econ Plann Sci 48(1):4–9

Bogetoft P, Heinesen E, Tranaes T (2015) The efficiency of educational production: a comparison of the Nordic countries with other OECD countries. Econ Model 50(C):310–321

Borge LE, Naper LR (2005) Efficiency potential and efficiency variation in Norwegian lower secondary schools. CESifo Working paper no 1624

Burney NA, Johnes J, Al-Enezi M, Al-Musallam M (2010) An assessment of efficiency of public schools in Kuwait using data envelopment approach (DEA) and Tobit regression. J Dev Econ Pol 12(2):7–33

Chakraborty K, Biswas B, Lewis WC (2001) Measurement of technical efficiency in public education: a stochastic and non stochastic production function approach. South Econ J 67 (4):889–905

Charnes A, Cooper WW, Rhodes E (1978) Measuring the efficiency of decision making units. Eur J Oper Res 2:429–444

Charnes A, Cooper WW, Rhodes E (1981) Evaluating program and managerial efficiency: an application of DEA to program follow-through. Manage Sci 27(6):668–697

Cherchye L, Witte KD, Ooghe E, Nicaise I (2010) Efficiency and equity in private and public education: a nonparametric comparison. Eur J Oper Res 202(2):563–573

Coelli TJ, Rao DSP, Battese GE (1998) An introduction to efficiency and productivity analysis. Kluwer Academic Publishers, Boston

Cuellar S, Felipe A (2014) The efficiency of education expenditure in Latin America and lessons for Colombia, Desarro. soc. 2014, n. 74, pp. 19–67. ISSN 0120-3584. http://dx.doi.org/10.13043/DYS.74.1

Cunha M, Rocha V (2012) On the efficiency of public higher education institutions in Portugal: an exploratory study. FEP Working paper No. 468, September 2012

Debreu E (1951) The coefficient of resource utilization. Econometrica 19(3):273–292

Farrell MJ (1957) The measurement of productive efficiency. J Royal Statis Soc 120(3):253–281

Fernando BIS, Emilyn CC (2007) Measuring efficiency and productive performance of colleges at the University of Santo Tomas: a nonparametric approach. Int Trans Oper Res 14(3):217–229

Ferrari G, Laurite T (2005) Evaluating technical efficiency of human capital formation in the Italian university: evidence from Florence. Stat Meth Appl 14(2):243–270

Flegg AT, Allen DO, Field AK, Thurlow TW (2004) Measuring the efficiency of British Universities: a multi-period data envelopment analysis. Educ Econ 12(3):231–249

Foltz JD, Barham BL, Chavas JP, Kim K (2012) Efficiency and technological change at US research universities. J Prod Anal 37(2):171–186

Grosskopf S, Hayes KJ, Taylor LL (2014) Efficiency in education: research and implications. Appl Econ Persp Policy 36(2):175–210

Haung CJ, Liu JT (1994) Estimation of non-neutral frontier production function. J Prod Anal 5 (2):171–180

Johnes J (2006a) Measuring efficiency: a comparison of multilevel modeling and data envelopment analysis in the context of higher education. Bull Econ Res 58(2):75–104

Johnes J (2006b) Data envelopment analysis and its application to the measurement of efficiency in higher education. Econ Educ Rev 25(3):273–288

Johnes J (2008) Efficiency and productivity change in the English higher education sector from 1996/97 to 2004/05. The Manchester School 76(6):653–674

Johnes J (2014) Efficiency and merger in English higher education 1996/97 to 2008/09: parametric and non- parametric estimation of the multi-input multi-output distance function. The Manchester School 82(4):465–487

Koopmans TC (1951) An analysis of production as an efficient combination of Activities. In: Koopmans TC (eds) Activity analysis of production and allocation. Cowles Commission for Research in Economics, Monograph no 13. Wiley, New York

Kumbhakar SC, Lovell CAK (2000) Stochastic frontier analysis. Cambridge University Press, Cambridge

Kingdon G (1996) The quality and efficiency of private and public education: a case study of Urban India. Oxford Bull Econ Stat 58(1):57–82

Kirjavainen T (2012) Efficiency of finnish general upper secondary schools: an application of stochastic frontier analysis with panel data. Educ Econ 20(4):343–364

Lassibilie G, Tan J (2001) Are private schools more efficient than public schools? Evidence from Tanzania. Educ Econ 9(2):145–172

Lovell CAK (1993) Production frontiers and productive efficiency. in Fried HO

Lovell CAK, Schmidt SS (eds) The measurement of productive efficiency: techniques and applications. Oxford University Press, New York

Lundvall K, Battese GE (2000) Firm size, age and efficiency: evidence from Kenyan manufacturing firms. J Dev Stud 36(3):146–163

Manceb [bacute] MJ, Bandres E (1999) Efficiency evaluation in secondary schools: the key role of model specification and of ex post analysis of results. Educ Econ 7(2):131–152

McMillan ML, Chan WH (2006) University efficiency: a comparison and consolidation of results from stochastic and non-stochastic methods. Educ Econ 14(1):1–30

Meeusen W, van den Broeck J (1977) Efficiency estimation from Cobb-Douglas production functions with composed error. Int Econ Rev 18(2):435–444

Mizala A, Romaguera P, Farren D (2002) The technical efficiency of schools in Chile. Appl Econ 34(12):1533–1552

Naper LR (2010) Teacher hiring practices and educational efficiency. Econ Educ Rev 29(4): 658–668

Ng YC, Li SK (2000) Measuring the research performance of Chinese higher education institutions: an application of data envelopment analysis. Educ Econ 8(2):139–156

Oliveira MA, Santos C (2005) Assessing school efficiency in Portugal using FDH and bootstrapping. Appl Econ 37(8):957–968

Pastor JT, Ruiz JL, Sirvent I (2002) A statistical test for nested radial DEA models. Operations Research, 50(4):728–735

Pohl C, Kempkes G (2010) The efficiency of German universities – some evidence from nonparametric and parametric methods. Appl Econ 42(6):2063–2079

Purohit BC (2015) Efficiency in education sector: a case of Rajasthan State (India). Madras School of Economics Working paper 121/2015

Ray SC (1991) Resource-use efficiency in public schools: a study of connecticut data. Manage Sci 37(12):1620–1628

Ray SC (2004) Data envelopment analysis: theory and techniques for economics and operations research. Cambridge University Press, Cambridge

Sankar D (2007) Education system performance among Indian states: a public expenditure efficiency analysis using linear programming methods. Washington, DC: World Bank. http://documents.worldbank.org/curated/en/2007/01/8933943/education-system-performance-among-indian-states-public-expenditure-efficiency-analysis-using-linear-programming-methods

Sengupta A, Pal NP (2010) Primary education in India: delivery and outcome- a district level analysis based on DISE data. J Educ Plann Admin 24(1):5–21

Sengupta A, Pal NP (2012) Assessing the primary schools multi-dimensional approach: a school level analysis based on indian data. Int J Educ Dev 32(2):264–272

Simar L, Wilson PW (2004) Performance of the bootstrap for DEA estimators and iterating the principle. In: Cooper WW, Seiford LM, Zhu J (eds) Handbook on data envelopment analysis. Kluwer Academic Publishers, Boston, pp 265–298 (Chapter 10)

Simar L, Wilson PW (2000) Statistical inference in nonparametric frontier models: The state of the art. J Prod Anal 13(1):49–78

Simar L, Wilson PW (2007) Estimation and inference in two-stage, semi-parametric models of productive efficiency. J Econ 136(1):31–64

Stevenson RE (1980) Likelihood functions for generalized stochastic frontier estimation. J Econ 13(1):57–66

Thanassoulis E, Portela MCAS (2002) School outcomes: sharing the responsibility between pupil and school. Educ Econ 10(2):183–207

Tyagi P, Yadav SP, Singh SP (2009) Efficiency analysis of schools using DEA: a case study of Uttar Pradesh state in India. https://www.academia.edu/7539059/Efficiency_analysis_of_schools_using_DEA_A_case_study_of_Uttar_Pradesh_state_in_India

Wolszczak-Derlac J (2014) An evaluation and explanation of (in)efficiency in higher education institutions in Europe and the U.S. with the application of two-stage semi-parametric DEA. IRLE Working Paper No. 114-14. http://irle.berkeley.edu/workingpapers/114-14.pdf

Chapter 3
The Output Oriented Measures of Technical Efficiency and Its Determinants in Primary and Upper Primary Level of Education in India

Abstract Output-oriented technical-efficiency (OUTTE) of primary, upper-primary education for General-Category-States (GCS), Special-Category-States (SCS) and Union-territories (UT) of India using non-parametric Data-Envelopment Analysis (DEA) is estimated, creating two frontiers for GCS, SCS&UT over 2005–06 to 2010–11. Net-enrolment-ratio, percentage of students getting 60 % marks and above are outputs; number of schools per-lakh population, teacher-pupil ratio, classroom-student ratio, percentages of teachers with qualification graduate and above are inputs representing quality for both output-input. Most of the States/UT is technically inefficient; output can increase with same input-usage. OUTTE of not all the states/UT has shown improved performance. Higher literacy-rate or educational-development-index does not imply better OUTTE. Second-stage panel-regression show the determinants OUTTE vary between category and level and highlight importance of policy, infrastructure and state-specific variables. OUTTE having regional variability is determined positively by the availability and utilization of central grant (AGM), ratio of girls to boys getting free text book, proportion of para-teachers among the total teachers in school, para-teacher's qualification; whether graduate and above, state's per-capita net-domestic-product-from-service-sector, density of population, percentage of school having drinking-water, common-toilet, getting school-development-grant, proportion of SC-teachers and SC-enrollment. Proportion of without-building-school, single-teacher-school, single-class-room-school, proportion of people below the poverty line, inequality in the distribution of income of the State has negative effect on OUTTE Both primary and upper-primary GCS-school has high technology-closeness-ratio implying maximum output producible from an input-bundle by a GCS-school is high compared to SCS&UT-school. It shows less benefit of a input-bundle from SCS&UT-school having greater elasticity of OUTTE with respect to AGM.

A. Ghose, *Efficiency of Elementary Education in India*,
SpringerBriefs in Economics, DOI 10.1007/978-81-322-3661-0_3

3.1 Introduction

The development of human capital in an economy is basically dependent on development of education sector. In India's National Development Programme, a substantial emphasis was given to the education sector. Among the different levels of education crucial is the development of elementary level of education. For attainment of equalization of education facilities across different States of India, an analysis of efficiency at the State level is needed. Such type of analysis will help us to identify the States that are lagging behind with respect to the Indian average in terms of efficiency and also to formulate appropriate policies for enhancing educational efficiency of those less efficient States in order to ensure equalization of educational efficiency across different States.

This chapter is concerned with the estimation of Output oriented technical efficiency score (OUTTE) of both primary and upper primary level of education. The concept of OUTTE is explained in Chap. 2. The major departure of this study from the existing literature is that first of all, while estimating OUTTE the frontier will not be constructed encompassing all the states and union territories, rather two frontiers one for General Category States (GCS) and the other for Special Category State and Union Territories (SCS&UT) will be constructed separately. The reason behind the construction of the two frontiers has already been explained in Chap. 1. Secondly, it carries out the group frontier and Meta frontier analysis. The Meta frontier defines the frontier corresponding to all the 35 states and union territories taken together. In particular, Technology Closeness Ratio (TCR) is computed showing the divergence of the group frontiers from the Meta frontiers, to see to what extent group frontiers are close to the Meta frontiers *and measuring whether, maximum educational–output producible from an input bundle by a school located in a particular group of state is as high as what could be produced if the school belongs to the other group. Such a computation will help us to identify whether the maximum output producible by SCS&UT is higher than that could be produced under GCS*, given the resources. Thirdly, while estimating TE it takes into account both quantities as well as quality aspects of output and inputs. The earlier studies dealing with interstate variation of technical efficiency score did not take into account the quality aspects. Fourthly, estimation of separate efficiency score for primary and upper primary level of education for different states of India and also its temporal variation is practically lacking. The present chapter measures OUTTE of both primary and upper primary level of education for six successive years from 2005–06 to 2010–11, under the assumption of variable returns to scale, to see how OUTTE have changed over time for different states and union territories and hence compares interstate efficiency performance of primary and upper primary level of education in India. Fifthly, since in the Indian context some data are available depicting a measure of educational development index (EDI). (Source National University of Educational Planning and Administration, NUEPA) it is examined whether the States/union territories with either high literacy rate or EDI are also the states with high technical efficiency. Finally, while finding out the determinants of

OUTTE, it takes account (i) some factors from poor infrastructure to see whether poor infrastructure inhibit the achievement of OUTTE, (ii) some factor from the favourable infrastructure to see whether availability of favourable infrastructure promotes TE. (iii) some social indicators to investigate whether inclusion of the backward classes into the education system increases OUTTE, (iv) some policy variables to test whether provision of more public facilities increases OUTTE and also (v) some state level macro aggregates like per-capita net State domestic product, income inequality, and number of persons below the poverty line to see to what extent the general environment of the state matters in explaining OUTTE. Also, rather than using a composite index the present chapter finds out the individual effect of the different explanatory variables. The earlier result that social and policy indicators are not significantly related to the efficiency improvement may be due to the use of composite index. It is quite possible that some of the individual factors comprising of the composite variable are significant while the others are not. *The present chapter also measures the relative sensitivity of the central-grant in explaining the efficiency performance of primary and upper-primary education of both GCS and SCS&UT. This relative sensitivity can be used for judging the efficacy of central grant in promoting technical efficiency of these two groups, the estimates of which are lacking in the literature.*

The chapter unfolds as follows. Section 3.2 deals with Methodology and data sources. Section 3.2.1 deals with the methodology for estimation of OUTTE. Sections 3.2.1.1 and 3.2.1.2 represent the process of estimation of OUTTE using group frontiers, Meta frontier and technology closeness ratio respectively. Section 3.2.2 represents the methodology for finding out the determinants of technical efficiency score for each group GCS, SCS&UT. Section 3.2.3 describes data sources. The empirical findings are presented in Sect. 3.3. Section 3.3.1 presents estimated results on OUTTE at primary level of education both for GCS, SCS&UT; Sects. 3.3.1.1 and 3.3.1.2 represent the estimated results on OUTTE for GCS, SCS&UT respectively. Section 3.3.2 presents estimated results on OUTTE at upper primary level of education both for GCS, SCS&UT; Sects. 3.3.2.1 and 3.3.2.2 represent the estimated results on output oriented TE score for GCS, SCS&UT respectively. Section 3.3.3 represents the comparison of literacy rate, OUTTE and educational development index. Section 3.3.4 represents estimated results on Technology Closeness Ratio (TCR). Section 3.4 represents analysis of the factors behind the variation of OUTTE at the primary level; Sects. 3.4.1 and 3.4.2 represent the factors behind the variation of OUTTE at primary level for GCS, SCS&UT respectively. Section 3.5 represents analysis of the factors behind the variation of OUTTE at the upper primary level; Sects. 3.5.1 and 3.5.2 represent the factors behind the variation of OUTTE at upper primary level for GCS, SCS&UT respectively. Section 3.6 represents relative sensitivity of central grant in explaining output oriented efficiency score at primary and upper primary level of education for General Category States (GCS), Special Category States (SCS) and Union Territories (UT) in India. Section 3.7 concludes with some policy suggestions.

3.2 Methodology and Data Sources

3.2.1 Methodology for Estimation of Output Oriented Measure of Technical Efficiency

Educational achievement can be viewed as a production process, where inputs of resources are applied to the relatively "unfinished" child, and an output-pupil achievement results. The objective is to generate the maximum achievement using a given amount of school resources. Efficiency measurement basically rests on assumed production relationship between inputs and outputs.

Like other production system, education also has the production function showing the relationship between school or student inputs and a measure of school output.

In the literature, estimation of efficiency of a school is basically rests on assumed production relationship between input and outputs. Following Ray (2004) educational production function can be defined as: Y = A (X1…Xm,). Where Y is some measure of school output—for example, enrolment ratio and or marks obtained in standardised examination system. X1,….Xm are the variables measuring the school environment. The variables here would typically include the amount and quality of teaching services, the physical infrastructure or facilities of the school.

The term A can be thought of as a shift parameter, being a function of (i) I_1,…In, the variables representing favourable Infrastructure facilities that promote TE level, (ii) PR_1,….PRq, the variables representing the poor infrastructure facilities that can reduce TE level, (i) Zn,….Zp the variables representing environmental influences on learning outside the school—These variables take care of the general environment of learning that the students faces.

In efficiency analysis it is not assumed that the production unit always behaves optimally and hence they can operate inefficiently. Efficiency measurement is a two stage problem—In order to judge the performance of the production units, a benchmark production function has to be constructed which is called as frontier, and is supposed to be perfectly efficient. The method of comparing the observed performance of production unit with the postulated standard of perfect efficiency is the basic problem of measuring efficiency.

The efficiency of a Decision Making Unit (DMU) generally consists of two components: technical efficiency (TE) and allocative efficiency (AE). The concepts of technical and allocative efficiency are described in Chap. 2. These two measures are combined to give a measure of total economic efficiency. *The present study is concerned only with the measurement of TE.*

TE of a DMU can be measured either by (i) output-oriented measure or by (ii) input-oriented measure. Further, the production function can follow either constant returns to scale or variable returns to scale. These concepts and their measurement are also described in Chap. 2.

The present chapter is concerned with estimation of output oriented technical efficiency score assuming variable return to scale (VRS). The Chap. 4 of this book will be devoted to estimation of input oriented technical efficiency score.

3.2.1.1 The Group and Meta-Frontiers

It is necessary to recognize that all of the observed DMUs may not have access to the same frontier. A variety of geographical, institutional, or other factors may give rise to such a situation. Constructing a single production frontier based on all the data points would, in such cases, result in an inappropriate benchmark technology. A way to measure the impact of technological heterogeneity across groups is to construct a separate *group frontier* for each individual group alongside a single *grand* or *meta-frontier* that applies to DMU from all the groups.

In order to construct different production possibility sets for different groups, we first group the observed input-output bundles by categories i.e.; whether it belongs to GCS or SCS&UT of the corresponding DMUs. Suppose N DMUs are observed and these DMUs are classified, according to some criterion, into H number of distinct and exhaustive groups, gth group containing N_g number of DMUs $\left(N = \sum_{g=1}^{H} N_g\right)$. Define the index set of observations J = $\{1, 2, \ldots N\}$ and partition it into non-overlapping subsets

J_g = {j: DMU j belongs to group g; (g = 1, 2, … H)}.

In this case, the production possibility set for group g will be

$$T^g = \left\{(x, y) : x \geq \sum_{j \in J_g} \lambda_{gj} x^j; y \leq \sum_{j \in J_g} \lambda_{gj} y^j; \sum_{j \in J_g} \lambda_{gj} = 1; \lambda_{gj} \geq 0\}; \right\} (g = 1, 2, \ldots, H)$$

The set T^g is the free disposal convex hull of the observed input-output bundles of DMUs from group g. Suppose, that the observed input-output bundle of DMU k in group g is (x_g^k, y_g^k). A measure of the within-group (output-oriented) technical efficiency of the DMU k, is

$$TE_g^k = \frac{1}{\varphi_g^k}$$

where φ_g^k solves the following problem:

$$\left(P_g^k\right) \qquad \varphi_g^k = \max\ \varphi$$

$$s.t.\ \sum_{j \in j_g} \lambda_{gj} y_g^j \geq \varphi\ y_g^k;$$

$$\sum_{j \in j_g} \lambda_{gj} y_g^j \leq x_g^k; \sum_{j \in j_g} \lambda_{gj} = 1;$$

$$\lambda_{gj} \geq 0\,(j = 1, 2, \ldots\ldots\ldots, N_g);\ \varphi \text{ unrestricted}$$

The above LP problem is solved for each DMU k in the gth group.

Next we consider TE of the same DMU k from group g relative to a *grand* technological frontier, or what is called the *Meta frontier*. The *Metafrontier* is the outer envelope of all of the group frontiers. It consists of the boundary points of the free disposal convex hull of the input-output vector of *all DMU* in the sample. The *(grand) technical efficiency* of the DMU k from group g is measured as

$$TE_G^k = \frac{1}{\varphi_G^k}$$

where

$$\varphi_G^k = \max\ \varphi$$

$$s.t.\ \sum_{g=1}^{H}\sum_{j\in J_g}\lambda_{gj}y_g^j \geq \varphi\ y_g^k;$$

$$\sum_{g=1}^{H}\sum_{j\in J_g}\lambda_{gj}y_g^j \leq x_g^k; \sum_{g=1}^{H}\sum_{j\in J_g}\lambda_{gj} = 1;$$

$$\lambda_{gj} \geq 0\,(j = 1, 2, \ldots, N_g; g = 1, 2\ldots H);\quad \varphi \text{ Unrestricted}$$

In view of the fact that the grand production possibility set contains every *group* production possibility set, it is obvious that $\varphi_g^k \leq \varphi_G^k$ and, hence, $TE_g^k \geq TE_G^k$, for every k and g. In other words, DMUs cannot be more technically efficient when assessed against the *Meta-frontier* than when evaluated against a *group* frontier.

3.2.1.2 Technology Closeness Ratio

When, for any DMU k in group g, the group efficiency and the grand efficiency measures are close, one may argue that evaluated at the input bundle x_g^k, the relevant group frontier is close to the meta-frontier. Instead of evaluating the proximity of the group frontier to the meta-frontier at individual points, it is useful to get an overall measure of proximity for the group as a whole. For this, we first define an average technical efficiency of the DMUs in the group (i.e., relative to the group frontier) by the taking a geometric average of such individual technical efficiencies. For the group g this will be given by

$$TE_g(g) = \left(\prod_{k=1}^{N_g} TE_g^k\right)^{1/N_g}$$

Similarly, the average technical efficiency of group g, measured from the meta-frontier, will be

$$TE_G(g) = \left(\prod_{k=1}^{N_g} TE_G^k \right)^{1/N_g}$$

For group g, an overall measure of proximity of the group frontier to the meta-, frontier is its technology closeness ratio (TCR)

$$TCR(g) = \frac{TE_G(g)}{TE_g(g)}$$

TCR increases if the group frontier shifts towards the meta-frontier, ceteris paribus, and is bounded above by unity which would be realized if and only if group frontier coincides with the meta-frontier.

3.2.2 Methodology of Finding Out Determinants of Output Oriented Measure of Technical Efficiency Score of Each Group

After obtaining technical efficiency score a second stage panel regression is carried out for finding out the determinants of efficiency. Different explanatory variables considered in this study along with their expected sign of influence on the technical efficiency score can be visualized from Table 3.1.

This chapter estimates TE using variable returns to scale (VRS). The included *General Category States (GCS)* are, Andhra Pradesh (AP), Bihar (BI), Chhattisgarh (CHHA), Goa (GO), Gujrat (GU), Haryana (HA), Jharkhand (JH), Karnataka (KA), Kerala (KE), Madhya Pradesh (MP), Maharastra (MH), Orissa (OR), Punjab (PU), Rajasthan (RA), TamilNadu (TN), Uttar Pradesh (UP), West Bengal (WB).

The included *Special Category States (SCS) and Union Territories (UT)* are Andaman and Nicobar Islands (AN), Arunachal Pradesh (ARP), Assam (AS), Chandigarh (CHAN), Dadra & NagarHaveli (DN), Daman & Diu (DD), Delhi (DE), Himachal Pradesh (HP), Jammu & Kashmir (JK), Lakshadweep (LAK), Manipur (MANI), Meghalaya (MEGHA), Mizoram (MIZO), Nagaland (NAGA), Puduchery (PUDU), Sikim (SI), Tripura (TR), Uttarakhand (UTTA).

For empirical estimation the present chapter considers two *outputs* viz.

(i) Net enrolment ratio and (ii) percentage of students passed with 60 % in the examination. This variable measures achievement of quality output.

The *inputs* used in this study are as follows:

(i) Number of schools per lakh population, (ii) teacher-pupil ratio in the school (iii) classroom-student ratio in the school, (iv) percentages of teachers with

Table 3.1 Descriptions of the factors influencing technical efficiency score

Determinants category	Factors	Expected impacts (+/−)
Poor infrastructure Basic question: Does poor infrastructure negatively affects TE?	1. Proportions of schools without building	−
	2. Proportions of schools having no pucca building	−
	3. Proportion of classroom in "bad" condition	−
	4. Proportion of single classroom school	−
	5. Proportion of single teacher school	−
Social indicators Basic question: Does more inclusion of the backward classes into the education system increases TE?	1. Proportion of SC teacher to total teacher in schools	+
	2. Proportion of ST teacher to total teacher in schools	+
	3. Proportion of SC enrolment in schools	+
	4. Proportion of ST enrolment in schools	+
	5. Proportion of female teachers to male teacher in schools	+
	6. Proportion of girls enrolment to boys in schools	+
Policy indicators Basic question: Does provision of more public facilities increases TE?	1. Actual amount of grant received by the states from the centre and utilised for elementary education purposes	+
	2. Proportion of students getting free text books in schools	+
	3. Proportion of girls getting free text books to boys in schools	+
	4. Proportion of girls getting free stationary to boys in schools	+
	5. Proportion of schools received School development grant	+
	6. Proportion of schools received Teaching learning Material grant	+
Macro indicators Basic question: Does general economic environment of the state has something to do with its TE?	1. The number of the persons below the poverty line in the state/union territories	
	2. Inequality in distribution of income i.e., Gini coefficient in the state/union territories	+
	3. Per capita net state domestic product or its different component like:	+
	4. Per capita net state domestic product coming from service sector (SVSHR)	+
	5. Per capita net state domestic product coming from industrial sector (INSHR)	+
	1. Density of population in the state/union territories	+

(continued)

Table 3.1 (continued)

Determinants category	Factors	Expected impacts (+/−)
Regional variability Basic question: Does regional variability matters in explaining TE?	1. Three regional dummy for East (d1), West (d2) and South (d3) taking North as a base	
Favourable infrastructure Basic question: Does favourable infrastructure positively affects TE?	1. Percentage of primary schools with drinking water facility	+
	2. Percentage of primary schools with common toilet	+
	3. Percentage of primary schools with girls' toilet	+
	4. Proportion of para teachers in schools	+
	5. Proportion of para teachers with graduate and above among the total number of teachers It may be pointed out that due to lack of sufficient number of full time teachers many schools employ a significant number of para teachers. So the basic question is does the quality of para teachers matters? This chapter takes into account both the quantity as well as the quality of para teachers	+

qualification graduate and above in the school. This variable measures quality of the teacher input.

3.2.3 *The Data Sources*

This chapter considers secondary data from collected from "DISE Statistics (Elementary Education; State Report Cards)", for the six successive years: 2005–06, 2006–07, 2007–08 and 2008–09, 2009–10. This information is based on District Information System for Education (DISE) raw data which was developed by the National University of Educational Planning and Administration (NUEPA). The data for the net per capita state domestic product has been collected from Ministry of Statistics and Programme Implementation (MOSPI), Government of India, while Gini coefficient data are collected from the Planning Commission and the Office of the Registrar General and Census Commissioner. The data for number of persons belonging to below poverty line has been taken from the statistics released by Ministry of Food and Consumer Affairs, Government of India.

3.3 The Empirical Findings

3.3.1 Output Oriented Technical Efficiency Score at Primary Level of Education in India

The OUTTE score of different States and the UT are obtained on the basis of a computer program DEAP version 2.1, developed by Tim Coelli. The estimated results of TE obtained for both GCS, SCS&UT for primary level of education are presented in Tables 3.2 and 3.3 respectively.

3.3.1.1 Output Oriented Technical Efficiency Score (OUTTE) of Primary Level of Education for General Category States (GCS) in India

The results of estimation of OUTTE reveal that for General Category States (GCS) and for primary level, OUTTE is equal to one for every year under study for state KA suggesting that this state is fully technically efficient over all the years under the study. The grand average of the TE for all the states and all the years is 0.7902. The states having OUTTE higher than this grand average are AP, BI,

Table 3.2 OUTTE of primary level of education for different years: General Category States (GCS)

States	2005–06	2006–07	2007–08	2008–09	2009–10	2010–11	Average
AP	0.945	0.916	0.935	0.97	0.93	0.94	0.94
BI	1.000	1.000	0.669	0.691	0.83	0.84	0.84
CHHA	0.994	0.995	0.611	0.988	0.895	0.97	0.89
GO	0.606	0.686	0.699	0.762	0.68	0.69	0.68
GU	1.000	1.000	0.993	1	0.997	0.998	0.998
HA	0.546	0.579	0.723	0.755	0.64	0.65	0.65
JH	0.757	0.494	0.770	1	0.74	0.76	0.75
KA	1.000	1.000	1.000	1	1.00	1.00	1
KE	1.000	0.999	1.000	1	0.58	1.00	0.99
MP	1.000	0.509	0.560	0.311	0.58	0.60	0.59
MH	1.000	0.914	0.917	0.987	0.96	0.97	0.958
OR	1.000	0.724	0.962	0.965	0.913	0.912	0.913
PU	0.585	0.560	0.579	0.619	0.584	0.585	0.585
RA	0.951	0.894	0.886	0.76	0.875	0.874	0.873
TN	1.000	1.000	0.993	1	0.996	0.997	0.998
UP	1.000	0.532	0.577	0.596	0.675	0.674	0.676
WB	0.977	0.876	0.867	0.857	0.894	0.896	0.894
Grand average							0.7902

Table 3.3 OUTTE of primary level of education for different years: Special Category States and Union Territories (SCS&UT)

States/UT	2005–06	2006–07	2007–08	2008–09	2009–10	2010–11	Average
AN	0.769	0.987	0.924	0.800	0.86	0.87	0.8683
ARP	0.431	0.541	0.643	0.345	0.48	0.49	0.4883
AS	1.000	0.934	0.835	1.000	0.941	0.942	0.942
CHAN	1.000	1.000	1.000	1.000	1.00	1.00	1.00
DN	1.000	1.000	1.000	1.000	1.00	1.00	1.00
DD	1.000	1.000	0.771	1.000	0.942	0.943	0.9425
DE	1.000	1.000	0.975	1.000	0.995	0.994	0.994
HP	1.000	1.000	0.982	0.979	0.980	0.99	0.9885
JK	0.880	0.894	0.897	1.000	0.92	0.918	0.918
LAK	1.000	1.000	1.000	1.000	1.00	1.00	1.00
MANI	0.551	0.595	0.715	0.426	0.573	0.572	0.572
MEGHA	1.000	0.459	0.519	0.405	0.597	0.596	0.572
MIZO	0.785	0.640	0.778	0.463	0.665	0.606	0.6651
NAGA	0.575	0.718	0.619	0.511	0.616	0.606	0.6075
PUDU	0.975	1.000	0.914	1.000	0.973	0.972	0.9723
SI	1.000	0.960	1.000	1.000	0.980	0.99	0.9883
TR	1.000	1.000	1.000	1.000	1.00	1.00	1.00
UTTA	0.887	0.823	0.973	0.982	0.926	0.926	0.917
Grand average							0.8588

CHHA, GU, KA, KE, MH, OR, TN and WB. The lowest average value of OUTTE occurs for the state PU (0.585). The level of OUTTE has declined over the year for the states BI, CHHA, GU, MH, OR, RA, TN and WB; has increased for HA and remained more or less stagnated for AP.

3.3.1.2 Output Oriented Technical Efficiency Score (OUTTE) of Primary Level of Education for Special Category States (SCS) and Union Territories (UT) in India

For the special category states and union territories (SCS&UT) and for the primary level OUTTE is equal to one for every year under the study for four states CHAN, DN, LAKH and TR. The grand average level of OUTTE for all the years and all the states is 0.8588. The states having higher level of OUTTE as compared to the grand average are AN, AS, CHAN, DN, DD, DE, HP, JK, LAK, PUDU, SI, TR and UTTA. The level of OUTTE has increased for AN, MANI, NAGA and UTTA, has declined for the states AS, DD, HP, MEGHA, MIZO, SI and more or less stagnated for ARP and PUDU. The average level of OUTTE; the average being taken over all the years is at minimum for ARP (0.4883).

3.3.2 Output Oriented Technical Efficiency Score (OUTTE) of Upper Primary Level of Education in India

The estimated results of OUTTE obtained for both GCS, SCS&UT for upper primary level of education are presented in Tables 3.4 and 3.5 respectively.

3.3.2.1 Output Oriented Technical Efficiency Score (OUTTE) of Upper Primary Level of Education for General Category States (GCS) in India

For GCS and upper primary level, OUTTE score is equal to one for all the years for AP and KE showing that these two states are fully technically efficient. The grand average level of OUTTE for all the years and all the General Category states turned out to be 0.7708. The level of OUTTE is higher than the grand average level for AP, GU, JK, KA, MH, RA, TN and WB. The level of OUTTE has increased under the period of study for GO, GU, HA, JH, OR, PU, UP and WB, has declined for the states BI, CHHA, KA, MH, RA and TN and remain more or less stagnated for MP. The average level of OUTTE; the average being taken over all the years is at minimum for the state GO (0.5711).

Table 3.4 OUTTE of upper primary level of education for different years: General Category States (GCS)

States	2005–06	2006–07	2007–08	2008–09	2009–10	2010–11	Average
AP	1.000	1.000	1.000	1.000	1.000	1.000	1.000
BI	1.000	1.000	0.954	1.000	1.000	1.000	1.000
CHHA	0.838	0.583	0.600	0.734	0.68	0.69	0.68
GO	0.446	0.679	0.582	0.606	0.58	0.57	0.5711
GU	0.865	0.795	0.998	1.000	0.92	0.91	0.9117
HA	0.294	0.659	1.000	1.000	0.74	0.73	0.7367
JH	0.442	0.712	0.694	0.974	0.71	0.70	0.7033
KA	1.000	0.970	1.000	1.000	0.98	0.99	0.99
KE	0.998	1.000	1.000	1.000	1.000	1.000	1.000
MP	0.729	0.751	0.678	0.730	0.73	0.72	0.7216
MH	1.000	0.985	0.971	1.000	0.98	0.99	0.9866
OR	0.442	0.461	0.962	0.677	0.64	0.63	0.6333
PU	0.520	0.690	0.641	0.953	0.690	0.701	0.6985
RA	1.000	0.897	0.941	0.951	0.945	0.947	0.9468
TN	1.000	0.971	0.987	1.000	0.98	0.99	0.988
UP	0.593	0.602	0.668	0.753	0.66	0.654	0.6545
WB	0.777	0.791	0.766	0.848	0.796	0.795	0.7955
Grand average							0.7708

3.3.2.2 Output Oriented Technical Efficiency Score of Upper-Primary Level of Education for Special Category States (SCS) and Union Territories (UT) in India

For SCS&UT and upper primary level, it is found that for no States/UT the OUTTE score is equal to one for every year under the study. Thus no states/UT is fully technically efficient for the SCS&UT and upper primary group. The grand average of the TE for all the states/UT under SCS&UT and all the years for upper primary level turns out to be 0.8731. The states/UT having higher level of OUTTE as compared to this grand average are CHAN, DN, DE, HP, JK, LAK, MIZO, NAGA, PUDU and TR. The average level of OUTTE; the average being taken over all the years is at minimum for SI (0.5O5). The level of OUTTE has increased over the years for the states AS and PUDU, declined for the states AN, ARP, CHAN, DN, DD, DE, HP, JK, LAK, MEGHA, MIZO, NAGA, TR and UTTA, while it has remained more or less stagnated for MANI.

Table 3.5 OUTTE of upper primary level of education for different years: Special Category States (SCS) and Union Territories (UT)

States/UT	2005–06	2006–07	2007–08	2008–09	2009–10	2010–11	Average
AN	1.000	0.678	0.762	0.759	0.79	0.80	0.7982
ARP	1.000	0.768	0.848	0.943	0.88	0.89	0.8881
AS	0.657	0.721	0.808	0.916	0.78	0.775	0.776
CHAN	1.000	0.993	1.000	1.000	0.999	0.998	0.9983
DN	1.000	1.000	0.915	0.972	0.973	0.972	0.972
DD	1.000	0.800	0.758	0.851	0.853	0.852	0.852
DE	1.000	0.843	0.858	1.000	0.926	0.925	0.925
HP	1.000	0.982	0.992	1.000	0.995	0.994	0.9938
JK	1.000	0.823	0.853	0.963	0.920	0.910	0.9115
LAK	1.000	1.000	0.965	1.000	0.992	0.991	0.9913
MANI	0.864	0.824	0.893	0.867	0.863	0.862	0.8621
MEGHA	0.883	0.527	0.674	0.649	0.693	0.683	0.6848
MIZO	0.994	0.773	0.896	1.000	0.926	0.916	0.917
NAGA	0.967	0.992	0.868	0.895	0.940	0.930	0.932
PUDU	0.893	1.000	0.934	1.000	0.967	0.957	0.958
SI	0.707	0.397	0.459	0.451	0.514	0.504	0.505
TR	1.000	1.000	0.988	1.000	0.996	0.997	0.997
UTTA	0.812	0.632	0.764	0.811	0.756	0.755	0.755
Grand average							0.8731

3.3.3 Comparison of the Literacy Rate, Output Oriented Technical Efficiency and Educational Development Index in India

At this outset the question can be raised is that whether the States with high literacy rates are also the States with the high technical efficiency. The comparison of the literacy rate and the output oriented technical efficiency taking into account all the states/UT taken together can be made from Table 3.6.

3.3.3.1 Comparison of Literacy Rate and Output Oriented Technical Efficiency in India

At this outset the question can be raised whether the states with high literacy rates are the states with high OUTTE score. The comparison of the literacy rate and the technical efficiency can be made from Table 3.6.

Table 3.6 suggests that (i) the states having higher than the all India average literacy rate are AN, CHAN, DD, DE, GO, GU, HP, KE, LAK, MH, MANI, MIZO, NAGA, PUDU, SI, TN, TR, UTTA and (ii) the states having below all India average literacy rate are AP, ARP, AS, BI, CHHA, DN, HA, JK, JH, KA, MP, MEGHA, OR, PU, RA, UP and WB.

Figures presented in Table 3.6 also suggest that for primary level, (i) for AN, AP, AS, CHAN, CHHA, DN, DD, DE, GU, HP, JK, KA, KE, LAK, MH, OR, PUDU, RA, SI, TN, TR, UTTA and WB, the OUTTE is above the average figure as obtained by taking into account OUTTE of all the States/UT taken together and (ii) for ARP, BI, GO, HA, JH, MP, MANI, MEGHA, MIZO, NAGA, PU and UP the OUTTE is below that of average figure for all the States/UT taken together.

Therefore the comparison of OUTTE at the primary level and the literacy rate suggests that:

(i) although the States GO, MIZO and NAGA belongs to the group of the States having higher than average literacy rate as compared to all India level, the level of OUTTE for these States is less than that of the average figure for all the States and UT taken together. Thus States having higher level of literacy rate not necessarily higher level of OUTTE.

(ii) The States/UT namely ARP, BI, HA, JH, MP, MEGHA, PU and UP are with below average OUTTE and they also belongs to the group having below average literacy rate, implying that the performance of these States/UT are not good, both in terms of average literacy rate and average OUTTE. There is a possibility of expansion of both output level as well as literacy rate.

(iii) The States AP, AS, CHHA, DN, JK, KA, KE, OR, RA and WB correspond to the states having below average literacy rate, but they are performing well in terms of OUTTE and correspond to the group having above average OUTTE level.

Table 3.6 A comparison of literacy rate, educational development index and output oriented technical efficiency score

State/UT	Literacy rate as per 2011 census	Rank of literacy rate	Average (Av) Output Oriented Technical Efficiency Score (OUTTE)				Educational Development Index (EDI)			
			Av OUTTE for primary level	Rank of OUTTE for primary level	Av OUTTE for upper primary level	Av OTE for upper primary level	Av EDI for primary level	Rank of EDI for primary level	Av EDI for upper primary level	Rank of EDI for upper primary level
AN	86.27	10	0.8683	18	0.7982	20	0.6242	18	0.7185	12
AP	67.66	31	0.94	11	1.00	1	0.6495	11	0.733	9
ARP	66.95	34	0.4883	29	0.8881	17	0.4457	33	0.5127	32
AS	73.18	26	0.942	10	0.776	22	0.4485	32	0.5332	30
BI	63.82	35	0.84	19	0.9923	5	0.3782	35	0.381	35
CHAN	86.43	8	1.00	**1**	0.9983	2	0.6922	6	0.76	4
CHHA	71.04	27	0.89	16	0.68	28	0.5502	24	0.5635	26
DN	77.65	19	1	**1**	0.972	9	0.544	25	0.6287	23
DD	87.07	6	0.9425	9	0.852	19	0.6257	16	0.7245	10
DE	86.34	9	0.994	3	0.925	10	0.7307	2	0.7567	6
GO	87.4	5	0.68	21	0.5711	31	0.625	17	0.687	17
GU	79.31	18	0.998	2	0.9177	13	0.6665	8	0.7122	13
HA	76.64	22	0.65	24	0.7367	22	0.639	15	0.698	16
HP	83.78	11	0.9885	5	0.9938	4	0.6395	14	0.7347	7
JK	68.74	30	0.918	12	0.9115	16	0.5972	20	0.6687	18
JH	67.63	32	0.75	20	0.7033	25	0.4232	34	0.4585	33
KA	75.6	23	1	**1**	0.99	7	0.668	7	0.7345	8
KE	93.91	1	0.99	4	1	1	0.7115	4	0.8017	2
LAK	92.28	2	1	**1**	0.9913	6	0.709	5	0.7622	3

(continued)

Table 3.6 (continued)

State/UT	Literacy rate as per 2011 census	Rank of literacy rate	Average (Av) Output Oriented Technical Efficiency Score (OUTTE)				Educational Development Index (EDI)			
			Av OUTTE for primary level	Rank of OUTTE for primary level	Av OUTTE for upper primary level	Av OTE for upper primary level	Av EDI for primary level	Rank of EDI for primary level	Av EDI for upper primary level	Rank of EDI for upper primary level
MP	70.63	28	0.59	26	0.7216	24	0.5337	27	0.546	28
MH	82.91	12	0.958	8	0.9866	8	0.6455	13	0.7242	11
MANI	79.85	16	0.572	28	0.8621	18	0.517	29	0.6432	22
MEGHA	75.48	24	0.572	28	0.6848	27	0.5122	30	0.5465	27
MIZO	91.58	3	0.6651	23	0.917	15	0.6627	9	0.70175	15
NAGA	80.11	15	0.6075	25	0.932	12	0.5907	21	0.6197	24
OR	73.45	25	0.913	14	0.6333	30	0.5395	26	0.5182	31
PUDU	86.55	7	0.9723	7	0.958	10	0.752	1	0.807	1
PU	76.68	21	0.585	27	0.6985	26	0.6607	10	0.7045	14
RA	67.06	33	0.873	17	0.9468	11	0.563	22	0.652	21
SI	82.2	13	0.9883	6	0.505	31	0.6482	12	0.663	19
TN	80.33	14	0.998	2	0.988	8	0.7237	3	0.7575	5
TR	87.75	4	1	**1**	0.997	3	0.5315	28	0.58275	25
UP	69.72	29	0.676	22	0.6545	29	0.5605	23	0.543	29
UTTA	79.63	17	0.917	13	0.755	23	0.619	19	0.6585	20
WB	77.08	20	0.894	15	0.7955	20	0.5045	31	0.449	34
All India	78.65		0.8588		0.7708		0.5981		0.6482	

(iv) The States AN, CHAN, DD, DE, GU, HP, KE, LAK, MH, PUDU, SI, TN, TR and UTTA belongs to both above average literacy rate and OUTTE and hence performance of these States are really good in terms of both OUTTE score and literacy rate.

The comparison of OUTTE at the upper primary level and the literacy rate suggests that:

(i) for AN, DD, GO, MANI, SI, UTTA although the literacy rate is higher than that of all India average, OUTTE of these States at upper primary level are below that of the corresponding average. Hence there is some scope of expansion of output given the resource utilization for these states at upper primary level.
(ii) The other States namely AS, CHHA, HA, JH, MP, MEGHA, OR, PU, UP and WB having below average OUTTE; the average obtained by considering all the States/UT taken together, also belongs to the group having below all India average literacy rate, implying that performance of these States/UT are really bad, both in terms of average literacy rate and average OUTTE. There is a possibility of expansion of output given the resource utilization.
(iii) The States AP, ARP, BI, DN, JK, KA, RA although belongs to below average literacy rate but they are performing well in terms of OUTTE and corresponds to the group having above average OUTTE level; the average obtained by considering all the States/UT taken together.
(iv) The States CHAN, DE, GU, LAKH, MH, MIZO, NAGA, PUDU, TN and TR belongs to both above all India average literacy rate and average OUTTE the average obtained by considering all the States/UT taken together and hence performance of these states are really good in terms of both OUTTE as well as literacy rate.

3.3.3.2 Comparison of Educational Development Index and Output Oriented Technical Efficiency in India

In the Indian context some data are available depicting a measure of educational development index (EDI). (Source National University of Educational Planning and Administration, NUEPA) *Therefore the question can be raised whether the states with high EDI are the states with the high technical efficiency?* Table 3.6 can also be used for the comparison of the EDI and the output oriented technical efficiency score (OUTTE). Figures on educational development index (EDI) for the primary sectors reveal that (i) the States and the union territories for which EDI is higher than all India level are AN, AP, CHAN, DD, DE, GO, GU, HA, HP, KA, KE, LAK, MH, MIZO, PU, SI, TN and (ii) the States ARP, AS, BI, CHHA, DN, JK, JH, MP, MANI, MEGHA, NAGA, OR, RA, TR, UP, UTTA and WB correspond to below all India average EDI. Similarly, the States for which the level of TE score is greater than the average figure of all the States/UT taken together are AN, AP, AS,

CHAN, CHHA, DN, DD, DE, GU, HP, JK, KA, KE, LAK, MH, OR, PUDU, RA, SI, TN, TR, UTTA and WB; while it is less for ARP, BI, GO, HA, JH, MP, MANI, MEGHA, MIZO, NAGA, PU and UP.

Therefore, a comparison of EDI and average OUTTE reveals that, *at primary level*

(i) Although the states HA, GO, MIZO and PU have EDI level higher than that of the average level for all the States and UT taken together corresponding to primary level, the OUTTE of these states at primary level are below that of the average level of OUTTE for all the states and UT taken together, corresponding to primary level and hence there is some scope of expansion of output for these States/UT, given the resource utilisation.
(ii) Although the States AS, CHHA, DN, JK, JH, OR, RA, TR and WB belongs to below average EDI corresponding to primary level, but they are performing well in terms of OUTTE score and belongs to the group having above average OUTTE; the average OUTTE is obtained by all the States/UT taken together corresponding to the primary level.
(iii) The States ARP, BI, JH, MANI, MP, MEGHA, NAGA and UP belongs to the group of States having both below average EDI and OUTTE score. Thus performances of these States are really bad both in terms of EDI and average OUTTE score; the average OUTTE is obtained by all the States/UT taken together corresponding to the primary level. Thus, there is a possibility of expansion of both output level as well as EDI.
(iv) The States AN, AP, CHAN, DD, DE, GU, KA, HP, KE, LAK, MH, SI, TN, belongs to both above average OUTTE and EDI, the average OUTTE is obtained by all the States/UT taken together corresponding to the primary level and hence performance of these States are really good in terms of both OUTTE and EDI.

Comparison of EDI and TE reveals that at the upper primary level,

(i) Although the states AN, DD, GO, PU, UTTA correspond to the group having higher than EDI as compared to the average level of EDI for all the States and UT taken together corresponding to upper primary level, OUTTE for these States are below that of average level of OUTTE for all the states and UT taken together corresponding to upper primary and hence there is a scope of expansion of output for these states.
(ii) For the States ARP, BI, DN, JK, NAGA and TR, EDI is below average level but OUTTE is above average level, both the averages are taken for all the states and UT taken together corresponding to upper primary level. Thus given the constraint the performances of these states are good.
(iii) For the States AP, CHAN, DE, GO, GU, HP, JK, KA, KE, MH, MIZO, PUDU, RA and TN both the level of EDI and OUTTE are higher than the average level for all the states and UT taken together corresponding to upper primary level, and hence performance of these States are really good in terms of EDI as well as OUTTE.

(iv) The States AS, CHHA, HA, JH, MP, MANI, MEGHA, OR, UP and WB belongs to the group having less than average level of EDI as well as OUTTE, both the averages are taken for all the States and UT taken together corresponding to upper primary level. Thus performances of these states are really bad.

3.3.4 Analysis of Technology Closeness Ratio

Table 3.7 shows the results of each group-frontier analysis. A high value of Technology Closeness Ratio (TCR) for any group implies that, on average, the maximum output producible from an input bundle by a DMU within the particular group would be almost as high as what could be produced if the DMU is just a member of the whole set of States. This in turn implies only that there are no significant physical, legal, cultural or technological constraints that hinder productivity of the State for being within that particular group.

TCR corresponding GCS is high as compared to SCS&UT with respect to both primary and upper primary level of education. Thus, we are getting less output from the employment of average bundle of input in a school that is located in SCS&UT as compared to a school belonging to GCS.

SCS&UT have high group mean as compared to GCS for both primary and upper primary level. The high group mean of the SCS&UT show that as a group SCS&UT are performing well in terms of group benchmark but infrastructural constraints hindered efficient production, as compared to GCS.

SCS&UT primary shows second highest level of grand efficiency (0.77) whereas, the group efficiency of this category is found to be high as well (0.82). Thus TCR of this said category is not appears to be very low (0.9390). It shows that from average input bundle, a school in SC&UT primary at most produce only about 94 % of what would be feasible if the school had been situated elsewhere in India. On the other hand SCS&UT upper primary has a high value of average group efficiency (0.86), but a relatively low value for average grand efficiency (0.75) as compared to SCS&UT primary indicating that *SCS&UT upper primary group* behaves homogeneously and relatively poorly. The group efficiency for GCS is low as compared to SCS&UT both in case of primary and upper primary level showing that performance of GCS is not homogeneous among themselves and there exists heterogeneity in comparison to SCS&UT. Both *GCS primary and upper primary level* are more close to Meta but they possesses lower value of group efficiency, representing the higher degree of variability among them.

The analysis of group frontier and Meta frontier in turn suggests that TCR value ranges from 0.97 to 0.87, signifying that the group classification in fact matters while estimating OUTTE of elementary education and on average, the maximum output producible from an input bundle by a school within the particular group is *not almost as high as* what could be produced if the school could choose to locate anywhere in India.

Table 3.7 Grand mean output oriented technical efficiency, group mean technical efficiency and technology closeness ratio for different education level and for different category of states (Average of all the years under study)

Year	Group mean	Grand mean	TCR
GCS primary	0.81	0.79	0.9753
GCS upper-primary	0.80	0.76	0.95
SCS&UT primary	0.82	0.77	0.9390
SCS&UT upper-primary	0.86	0.75	0.8721

After obtaining OUTTE a second stage panel regression is resorted to for finding out the determinants for GCS, SCS and primary and upper primary level of education separately. The four panels consists of OUTTE score for (i) each of the 17 GCS for primary level, (ii) each of the 17 GCS for upper primary level, (iii) each of the 18 SCS&UT for primary and (iv) each of the 18 SCS&UT for upper primary level over the period 2005–06 to 2010–2011 along with the determinants variables for each of the panel. Different regressions are tried out and the best fit is reported. To test for appropriateness of the assumption of fixed effect *vis. a vis.* the random effect panel model, Haussmann's specification test is performed for each of the regressions which strongly rejects the assumption of fixed effect model in favour of random effect model. To take into account heterogeneity among the regions, dummy for the three regions East (d1), West (d2) and South (d3) is included in the regression taking North as a benchmark.

3.4 Analysis of the Factors Behind the Variation of Output Oriented Technical Efficiency Score at Primary Level of Education in India

Results of panel regression suggest that infrastructural variables, policy variables and school specific variables and also the level macro aggregates are important in explaining TE score for the primary level of education and for GCS and SCS and UT.

3.4.1 Factors Behind the Variation of Output Oriented Technical Efficiency Score (OUTTE) at Primary Level of Education for General Category States (GCS) in India

The results of estimation of the factors influencing the efficiency score of primary level of education for GCS are presented in Table 3.8.

The results of estimation suggest that in case of GCS Primary level, OUTTE is *first of all* negatively influenced by poor infrastructure. For example, poor

Table 3.8 Significant variables influencing OUTTE of GCS primary level

Variables	Coefficients	z-value	Goodness of fit of model
WBSP	−0.0074223	−3.25	Wald Chi^2 = 206.43
STSCP	−0.0014758	−2.10	P > Chi^2 = 0.0000
SCSCP	−0.23	−2.72	
AGMPG	0.1732598	2.38	
SSDGP	0.0067532	2.82	
BPL	−0.0000728	−3.32	
d2	0.1105913	2.17	
d3	0.3233842	5.84	
SVSHR	1.646667	4.51	
PTHP	0.16	2.28	
SFTBP	0.07	4.34	

infrastructure namely (i) proportion of primary school without building (WBSP) (ii) proportion of primary of school with single teacher (STSCP), (iii) proportion of primary school with single class room (SCSCP) negatively affects OUTTE. *Secondly,* OUTTE score is also influenced by the availability of human capital. For example OUTTE score is positively influenced by the proportion of para teachers in the primary school (PTHP), implying that the availability of para teachers is definitely important and significantly contributing to the OUTTE. *Thirdly,* policy variables are in fact important in explaining OUTTE score. For example, OUTTE score is positively and significantly influenced by the policy variables like actual utilization of received Central grant for primary education purposes by the GCS (AGMPG), availability of free text book, i.e., proportion of students getting free text book at the primary level (SFTBP), percentage of primary school received school development grant (SSDGP). *Finally,* the OUTTE score is also influenced by some State specific factors. For example, OUTTE is negatively and significantly influenced by proportion of people lying below the poverty line (BPL). The intuition behind this is that greater is the proportion of people below the poverty line lesser will be the chance that the family will send their child to the school and more will be the extent of drop out and hence less will be the magnitude of OUTTE. Similarly, the OUTTE also depends on per capita net state domestic product. In fact, per capita net state domestic product from the service sector (SVSHR) is a positive factor influencing the level of TE. Intuition behind this is that higher the state domestic product from the service sector, higher will be the income of the state and hence higher the chances that the family will send their child to the school and less will be the extent of drop out. Thus, higher will be the extent of OUTTE. Further, OUTTE is also influenced by the regional variability. The two regional dummy d2 for West and d3 for South taking North as benchmark are positive and statistically significant implying that the states from West and South are technically more efficient than North.

3.4.2 *Factors Behind the Variation of Output Oriented Efficiency Score (OUTTE) at Primary Level of Education for Special Category States (SCS) and Union Territories (UT) in India*

The results of estimation of the factors influencing the efficiency level of primary level of education for SCS&UT are presented in Table 3.9.

The results of estimation suggest that in case of *SCS&UT and the Primary level, OUTTE* is *first of all* negatively influenced by poor infrastructure. For example, poor infrastructure, namely (i) proportion of primary school without building (WBSP) (ii) proportion of primary of school with single teacher (STSCP) negatively affects OUTTE. At the same time, OUTTE level is also positively influenced by favourable infrastructure. For example, (i) proportion of primary school having drinking water facility (DRINKW) and (ii) proportion of primary school having common toilet (COMMONT) positively affects OUTTE level. *Secondly,* OUTTE is also influenced by the policy variables. For example, the policy variable likes (i) proportion of girls to boys getting free stationary (GBFSP), (ii) actual utilization of received grant from centre for primary education purposes by SCS&UT (AGMPS) positively influence OUTTE level. *Thirdly,* the state specific macro aggregate like proportion of the people lying below the poverty line (BPL) has a negative effect of OUTTE of the SCS&UT primary level of education, the argument for this has already been specified. *Finally,* the OUTTE is also affected by regional variability. The coefficients of two regional dummy variables d1 for East and d3 for South taking North as benchmark are positive and statistically significant implying that the states from East and South are technically more efficient than North.

Table 3.9 Significant variables influencing OUTTE of SCS&UT primary level of education

Variables	Coefficients	z-value	Goodness of fit of model
WBSP	−0.06	−3.51	Wald Chi^2 = 196.43
STSCP	−0.01	−2.20	P > Chi^2 = 0.0000
AGMPS	0.27	2.28	
GBFSP	0.067	2.75	
BPL	−0.072	−3.16	
d1	0.21	2.74	
d3	0.423	4.84	
DRINKW	0.26	3.51	
COMMONT	0.646	2.64	

3.5 Factors Behind the Variation of Output Oriented Efficiency Score at Upper Primary Level of Education in India

Results of panel regression suggest that infrastructural variables, policy variables and school specific variables and also the State level macro aggregates are important in explaining TE score for the Upper primary level of education and for GCS and SCS&UT.

3.5.1 Factors Behind the Variation of Output Oriented Technical Efficiency Score (OUTTE) at Upper Primary Level of Education for General Category States (GCS) in India

The results of estimation of the factors influencing the efficiency level of upper-primary level of education for GCS are presented in Table 3.10.

Considering the GCS school belonging to upper primary level, it is found that OUTTE is *first of all* negatively influenced by poor infrastructure. For example, proportion of upper primary school with single teacher (STSCUP) has a negative influence on the OUTTE level. *Secondly,* OUTTE level is also positively influenced by favourable infrastructure. For example, (i) proportion of upper primary school having drinking water facility (DRINKW) and (ii) proportion of upper primary school having common toilet (COMMONT) positively affects OUTTE level. *Secondly,* OUTTE score is also influenced positively by the availability of human capital. For example, the quality of para teachers is important and OUTTE score is positively influenced by the number of para teachers with qualification graduate degree and above (PTHQN). *Thirdly,* OUTTE score is also influenced by the policy

Table 3.10 Significant variables influencing OUTTE of GCS upper primary level of education

Variables	Coefficients	z-value	Goodness of fit of model
STSCUP	−0.006	−3.15	Wald Chi^2 = 146.48
DRINKW	0.007	2.80	P > Chi^2 = 0.0000
COMMONT	0.17	2.28	
AGMUPG	0.3510	2.56	
SSDGUP	0.0057	2.82	
GINI	−0.07	−2.32	
d2	0.210	2.87	
d3	0.42	4.84	
SVSHR	0.646667	3.61	
PTHQN	0.56	3.68	

variables. For example, policy variable like actual utilization of received central grant for upper primary purposes by the GCS (AGMUPG) has a positive influence on OUTTE The other policy variable which is important is the proportion of upper primary school received school development grant (SSDGUP). *Fourthly*, the State specific factor has some role to play in influencing TE score. For example, OUTTE is negatively influenced by inequality in the distribution of income as measured by Gini coefficient (GINI). The intuition behind this is that if the inequality in the distribution of income is high for any State, it is likely that access to education will be limited to fewer numbers of people. Thus higher the extent of inequality in the distribution of income for any particular State, lesser is the percentage of family sending their child to school, or the consequent drop out will be higher, which may have a negative influence on the OUTTE. Similarly, the OUTTE is positively influenced by per capita net state domestic product from the service sector (SVSHR). In fact, as argued above, the net domestic product from the service sector will have a favourable effect on OUTTE. *Finally*, there exists regional variability. The two regional dummy d2 for West and d3 for South taking North as benchmark are positive and statistically significant implying that the states from West and South are technically more efficient than North.

3.5.2 Factors Behind the Variation of Output Oriented Efficiency Score at Upper Primary Level of Education for Special Category States (SCS) and Union Territories (UT) in India

The results of estimation of the factors influencing the efficiency level of upper-primary level of education for SCS&UT are presented in Table 3.11.

The results of estimation suggest that in case of SCS and the upper primary level, OUTTE is *first of all* positively influenced by favourable infrastructure. For example, (i) percentage of upper primary school having drinking water facility (DRINKW) positively affects OUTTE score. *Secondly*, OUTTE is negatively influenced by poor

Table 3.11 Significant variables influencing OUTTE of SCS&UT upper primary level of education

Variables	Coefficients	z-value	Goodness of fit of model
WBSP	−0.005	−3.15	Wald Chi^2 = 162.34
STSCP	−0.006	−2.20	P > Chi^2 = 0.0000
AGMUPS	0.4520	2.76	
DRINKW	0.003	2.82	
GINI	−0.002	−3.26	
SCENUP	0.2105	2.27	
STSCUP	0.26	4.84	
POPDEN	1.646667	4.51	

infrastructure; proportion of upper primary school without building (WBSUP) and proportion of upper primary school with single teacher (STSCUP) negatively affects OUTTE. *Thirdly,* OUTTE score is positively influenced by proportion of SC teachers to total teachers (SCTHUP), proportion of SC enrolment to total enrolment (SCENUP) suggesting that inclusion of backward classes into the system in fact increases the efficiency score. *Thirdly,* OUTTE score is also influenced by the policy variables. For example, policy variable like actual utilization of received central grant for Upper primary education level corresponding to SCS&UT (AGMUPS) has a positive influence on OUTTE level. *Finally,* the state specific factor has some role to play in influencing OUTTE. For example, OUTTE score is negatively influenced by inequality in the distribution of income as measured by Gini coefficient (GINI). As justified above, higher the extent of inequality in the distribution of income for any particular state, lesser is the extent of TE level. Further, OUTTE level is also influenced by density of population. Higher the density of population higher is the level of OUTTE. It implies higher the value of POPDEN more the concentration of child population and hence economics of scale in-terms of provision of inputs results in the higher value of OUTTE.

3.6 Relative Sensitivity of Central Grant in Explaining Output Oriented Efficiency Score at Primary and Upper Primary Level of Education for General Category States (GCS), Special Category States (SCS) and Union Territories (UT) in India

One interesting thing that appears from the analysis is that OUTTE score of GCS primary, SCS&UT primary, GCS upper primary, SCS&UT upper primary level of education are significantly related to availability as well as utilisation of grant from Centre, the elasticity of OUTTE with respect to the grant variable for these four categories are 0.1355, 0.2609, 0.3314, 0.4380 respectively. Thus, the *elasticity of TE with respect to AGM is higher for the SCS&UT as compared to the GCS for both primary and upper primary level.*

Further, as expected elasticity of OUTTE with respect to the grant variable is higher in upper primary level as compared to primary level both in case of GCS and SCS&UT.

3.7 Conclusions

The present chapter thus postulates the following observation on TE for primary and upper primary level of education and for GCS and SCS&UT.

- The analysis of group frontier and Meta frontier suggests that the TCR value ranges from 0.87 to 0.97, signifying that the group classification in fact matters and on average, the maximum output producible from an input bundle by a school required within the region *is not almost as high as* what could be produced if the school could choose to locate anywhere in India.

- TCR corresponding GCS is high as compared to SCS&UT with respect to both primary and upper primary level of education. Thus, we are getting a less benefit from the employment of average bundle of input in a school that is located in a SCS&UT as compared to a school belonging to a GCS.
- The *group efficiency* for *GCS* is low as compared to SCS&UT both in case of *primary* and *upper primary*. Although both GCS primary and upper primary level are more close to Meta but *they possesses lower value of group efficiency, representing the higher degree of variability among them.*
- SCS Upper-Primary has a high value of average group efficiency, but a relatively low value for average Grand efficiency as compared to SCS primary indicating that in this group almost all schools behave homogeneously and relatively poorly as compared to *SCS Primary*!
- Results of panel regression suggest that infrastructural variables, policy variables and school specific variables and also the state level macro aggregates are important in explaining TE scores. This observation is true for both the primary and upper primary level of education and for GCS and SCS&UT. The result is different from the earlier result of Sengupta and Paul that social and policy indicators are not significantly related to the efficiency improvement.
- TE score of both GCS and SCS&UT and for primary and upper primary level of education are significantly related to availability as well as utilisation of actual grant from Centre (AGM). The *elasticity of OUTTE with respect to AGM is higher for the SCS&UT as compared to the GCS both in case of primary and upper primary level of education. Also elasticity of OUTTE score is higher for upper primary as compared to primary both in case of GCS and SCS&UT.*

References

Bhandari AK, Ray SC (2012) Technical efficiency in the Indian textiles industry: a non parametric analysis of firm level data. Bull Econ Res 64(1):109–124

Ray SC (2004) Data envelopment analysis: theory and techniques for economics and operations research. Cambridge University Press, Cambridge

Chapter 4
The Input Oriented Technical Efficiency and Its Determinants in Primary and Upper Primary Level of Education in India

Abstract This chapters estimates input-oriented technical-efficiency (INPTE) of primary, upper-primary education for General-Category-States (GCS), Special-Category-States (SCS) and Union-territories (UT) of India using non-parametric Data-Envelopment Analysis (DEA) creating two frontiers for GCS, SCS&UT over 2005–06 to 2010–11, explains its determinants employing second-stage panel regression and determines the extent of underutilization of inputs. Net-enrolment-ratio, percentage of students getting 60 % marks and above are outputs; number of schools per-lakh population (SPLP), teacher-pupil ratio (PTR), classroom-student ratio (CR), percentages of teachers with qualification graduate and above (TQ) are inputs; quality of both output and input is thus important. Most of the States/UT is technically inefficient; input can be contracted keeping output unchanged. INPTE of not all the States/UT has improved. Input-underutilization is highest for SPLP for three categories/levels and for TQ for one; is lowest for PTR for one category/level and TQ for three. The determinants vary across category/level, highlighting role of policy, infrastructure, social-indicator, state-specific variables and regional variability. The availability and utilization of central grant (AGM), ratio of girls to boys getting free text book, proportion of para-teachers with qualification graduate and above among the total number of teachers, state's per-capita net-domestic-product-from-service-sector, density-of-population, percentage of school having drinking-water, students getting free text book, proportion of SC teacher to total teacher have a positive effect, while inequality in the distribution of income, proportion of school without building have negative effect on INPTE. AGM has indirect effect through other variables. For SCS&UT-primary there is an optimum-AGM beyond which negative-effect of AGM on INPTE operates.

4.1 Introduction

For measuring performance of education sector it is necessary to measure whether the inputs used in the production process are used efficiently. The basic question is whether there is any room for greater efficiency?

A. Ghose, *Efficiency of Elementary Education in India*,
SpringerBriefs in Economics, DOI 10.1007/978-81-322-3661-0_4

In this context an analysis of input oriented technical efficiency at the State level is needed. This will help us to identify the States that are lagging behind with respect to the Indian average in terms of input oriented technical efficiency and also to formulate appropriate policies for efficiency level of those States.

The present chapter intends to measure the extent of input efficiency and also find out the factor influencing the variation of such efficiency. The analysis of *input oriented technical efficiency for the education sector is still lacking in the* literature. The contributions of the present chapter to the literature are the following. First of all, under the assumption of variable returns to scale it measures input oriented technical efficiency score (INPTE) of both primary as well as upper primary level of education for four successive years from 2005–06 to 2010–11. The chapter also finds out how the efficiency scores have changed over time. It also estimates underutilization of different inputs used in the production process for different states of India, if it exists at all. Secondly, while finding out the determinants of efficiency, it intends to take into account (i) some factors from poor infrastructure to see whether poor infrastructure inhibit the achievement of INPTE, (ii) some factors from favorable infrastructure to see whether favorable infrastructure facilitates the achievement of INPTE, (iii) some social indicators to investigate whether inclusion of the backward classes into the education system increases INPTE, (iv) some policy variables to test whether provision of more public facilities increases INPTE and also (v) some state level macro aggregates like per-capita net State domestic product, income inequality, and number of persons below the poverty line to see to what extent the general environment of the state matters in explaining INPTE. Also, rather than using a composite index the present paper attempts to find out the individual effect of the different explanatory variables. It is quite possible that some of the individual factors comprising of the composite variables are significant while the others are not.

The rest of the chapter unfolds as follows. Section 4.2 deals with Methodology and the data sources. Section 4.2.1 deals with the methodology for estimation of INPTE and Sect. 4.2.2 deals with data sources. The empirical findings are presented in Sect. 4.3. Section 4.3.1 presents estimated results on INPTE at primary level of education both for GCS and SCS&UT; Sects. 4.3.1.1 and 4.3.1.2 represent the estimated results on INPTE for GCS and SCS&UT respectively. Section 4.3.2 presents estimated results on INPTE at upper primary level of education both for GCS and SCS&UT; Sects. 4.3.2.1 and 4.3.2.2 represent the estimated results on INPTE for GCS and SCS&UT respectively. Section 4.3.3 represents radial and slack movements in inputs. Input slack and radial movement at primary and upper primary level of Education in India is presented in Sects. 4.3.3.1 and 4.3.3.2 respectively. The factors behind the variation of INPTE are presented in Sect. 4.4. Section 4.4.1 represents analysis of the factors behind the variation of INPTE at the primary level; Sects. 4.4.1.1 and 4.4.1.2 represent the factors behind the variation of INPTE at primary level for GCS and SCS&UT respectively. Section 4.4.2 represents analysis of the factors behind the variation of INPTE at the upper primary level; Sects. 4.4.2.1 and 4.4.2.2 represent the factors behind the variation of INPTE at upper primary level for GCS and SCS&UT respectively. Section 4.5 concludes with some policy suggestions.

4.2 Methodology and Data Source

This chapter uses two stage methodologies. In the first stage, the input oriented technical efficiency (TE) of the Decision Making Unit (DMU) is computed using the Data Envelopment Analysis (DEA). The extent of underutilization of different inputs used in the production process for different states of India if at all it exists is measured. The estimated input oriented technical efficiency score is then used to find out its determinants using a second stage panel regression.

4.2.1 *Measurement of Input Oriented Technical Efficiency (TE)*

The methodology for finding out input oriented measure of technical efficiency (INPTE) using Data Envelopment Approach is explained in Chap. 2. The measurement of INPTE necessitates the assumption of some kind of production function relationship between the input and output for education sector. The assumed production function relationship is same as in Chap. 3.

The INPTE estimated in the chapter is a radial measure. Thus if there is any inefficiency, it can be measured by taking a radial contraction of the input on to the frontier. However, all the inputs used are not potentially reduced. The horizontal or vertical portion of an isoquant also accounts for inefficiency in usage of inputs and is known as input slack. Thus there may be the possibility of the existence of input slack for the case of multiple input production process. One advantage of using Data Envelopment Analysis is that it is possible to compute input slack. The concept and the method of estimation of the slack movement is also explained in Chap. 2. The extent of underutilization of input is therefore is the sum of radial and slack movement taken together.

4.2.2 *Data Source*

The included General Category state (GCS), Special Category States (SCS) and Union Territories (UT), the variable used as well as the sources of the data is same as in Chap. 3.

4.3 The Empirical Findings

The INPTE score of the different states and the UT, the input slack and radial movement for different inputs are obtained on the basis of a computer program DEAP Version 2.1, developed by Tim Coelli.

4.3.1 Input Oriented Technical Efficiency Score (INPTE) at Primary Level of Education in India

The estimated results of INPTE for GCS primary level of education is presented in Table 4.1.

4.3.1.1 INPTE of Primary Level of Education for General Category States (GCS) in India

The figures presented in Table 4.1 reveal that for GCS and for primary level INPTE is equal to one for every year under the study for the states BI, KA and JH suggesting that these three states are fully technically efficient over all the years under the study. The level of TE is not equal to one for only one year 2006–07 in case of KE and for 2007–08 in case of GU and TN. The minimum level of INPTE occurs for MP (0.493). The grand average level of INPTE for all the years and all the States taken together is 0.8066. The States/UT having higher than this grand average are AP, BI, GU, JH, KA, KE, MH, OR, TN and WB. The States/UT having less than this grand average are CHHA, GO, HA, MP, OR, PU, RA and UP. The level of INPTE has declined for CHHA, GO, HA, MP, OR, PU, RA, UP and WB, while it has increased for AP and remains unchanged for GO.

Table 4.1 INPTE of primary level of education for General Category States (GCS) in India

State	2005–06	2006–07	2007–08	2008–09	2009–10	2010–11	Average
AP	0.870	0.684	0.671	1.000	1.00	1.00	0.8708
BI	1.000	1.000	1.000	1.000	1.00	1.00	1
CHHA	0.970	0.732	0.443	0.606	0.605	0.609	0.6608
GO	0.770	0.771	0.716	0.773	0.778	0.780	0.7646
GU	1.000	1.000	0.961	1.000	1.00	1.00	0.9935
HA	0.880	0.644	0.614	0.573	0.576	0.579	0.6443
JH	1.000	1.000	1.000	1.000	1.00	1.00	1.00
KA	1.000	1.000	1.000	1.000	1.00	1.00	1.00
KE	1.000	0.997	1.000	1.000	1.00	1.00	0.9995
MP	1.000	0.500	0.385	0.351	0.354	0.358	0.4913
MH	1.000	0.760	0.692	1.000	1.00	1.00	0.9086
OR	1.000	0.716	0.952	0.669	0.672	0.674	0.7805
PU	0.752	0.586	0.606	0.537	0.539	0.542	0.5936
RA	0.901	0.500	0.500	0.500	0.505	0.509	0.58
TN	1.000	1.000	0.974	1.000	1.00	1.00	0.9956
UP	1.000	0.538	0.514	0.500	0.516	0.518	0.5976
WB	0.961	0.774	0.749	0.680	0.689	0.691	0.8225
Grand average							0.8060

4.3.1.2 Input Oriented Technical Efficiency Score (INPTE) of Primary Level of Education for Special Category States (SCS) and Union Territories (UT) in India

The estimated results of INPTE for SCS and UT primary level are given in Table 4.2.

The figures on Table 4.2 suggests that for SCS&UT and for primary level, INPTE is equal to one for every year under the study for the States/UT like CHAN, LAK and TR implying that these three States/UT are fully technically efficient over all the years under the study. The level of TE is equal to one except for the year 2006–07 in case of SI and for the year 2007–08 in case of three States/UT namely DN, DD and DE. The minimum level of INPTE for all the years and all the States taken together is 0.5521 and it happened for the state ARP. The grand average level of INPTE for all the years and all the states taken together turned out to be 0.8419. The States/UT having higher than grand average are AS, CHAN, DN, DD, HP, LAK, PUDU, SI and TR. On the other hand States/UT having TE below that of grand average are ARP, JK, MANI, MEGHA, MIZO, NAGA and UTTA. The level of INPTE has declined for AN, ARP, HP, MEGHA and NAGA. INPTE has increased for JK, MIZO and PUDU; and remains more or less stagnated for MANI.

Table 4.2 INPTE of primary level of education for Special Category States (SCS) and Union Territories (UT) in India

State/UT	2005–06	2006–07	2007–08	2008–09	2009–10	2010–11	Average
AN	0.826	0.866	0.807	0.715	0.717	0.720	0.7751
ARP	0.717	0.508	0.491	0.531	0.532	0.534	0.5521
AS	1.000	0.983	0.949	1.000	1.00	1.00	0.9886
CHAN	1.000	1.000	1.000	1.000	1.00	1.00	1
DN	1.000	1.000	0.987	1.000	1.00	1.00	0.9978
DD	1.000	1.000	0.823	1.000	1.00	1.00	0.9705
DE	1.000	1.000	0.973	1.000	1.00	1.00	0.9955
HP	1.000	1.000	0.867	0.767	0.769	0.771	0.8623
JK	0.509	0.677	0.675	1.000	1.00	1.00	0.8101
LAK	1.000	1.000	1.000	1.000	1.00	1.00	1
MANI	0.592	0.513	0.554	0.599	0.597	0.598	0.5755
MEGHA	1.000	0.555	0.592	0.599	0.594	0.596	0.656
MIZO	0.686	0.554	0.693	0.732	0.734	0.733	0.6887
NAGA	0.713	0.661	0.618	0.649	0.645	0.648	0.6557
PUDU	0.863	1.000	0.826	1.000	1.00	1.00	0.9481
SI	1.000	0.710	1.000	1.000	1.00	1.00	0.9516
TR	1.000	1.000	1.000	1.000	1.00	1.00	1
UTTA	0.528	0.435	0.710	0.899	0.897	0.898	0.7278
Grand average							0.8419

4.3.2 *Input Oriented Technical Efficiency Score (INPTE) of Upper Primary Level of Education in India*

4.3.2.1 INPTE of Upper Primary Level of Education for General Category States (GCS) in India

Table 4.3 presents the estimated results of INPTE for GCS upper primary level.

The figures presented in Table 4.4 suggests that for GCS upper primary level, INPTE is equal to one for every year under the study for AP, BI, MH, and RA suggesting that these four states are fully technically efficient over this entire period. The level of INPTE is not equal to one (i) for 2 years 2005–2006 and 2006–07 in case of GU; 2006–07 and 2007–08 in case of TN; (ii) for one year 2007–08 in case of JH; for 2006–07 in case of KA; for 2005–06 in case of KE, PU and HA. Therefore, the states GU, JH, KA, KE, PU and TN although are not perfectly efficient for each of the year, INPTE of these states are in fact quiet high. The minimum value of INPTE occurs for PU. The grand average TE level for all the years and all the states taken together turns out to be 0.8806. The States for which INPTE higher than grand average are AP, BI, GU, HA, JH, KA, KE, MH, PU, RA and TN. The States having INPTE lower than this grand average are CHHA, GO, MP, OR, UP and WB. The level of INPTE has increased for GO, GU, HA, OR, PU and WB, while it has declined for CHHA and MP.

Table 4.3 INPTE of upper primary level of education for General Category States (GCS) in India

State	2005–06	2006–07	2007–08	2008–09	2009–10	2010–11	Average
AP	1.000	1.000	1.000	1.000	1.00	1.00	1
BI	1.000	1.000	1.000	1.000	1.00	1.00	1
CHHA	0.777	0.469	0.406	0.755	0.753	0.756	0.6526
GO	0.474	1.000	0.408	0.497	0.498	0.510	0.5645
GU	0.750	0.807	1.000	1.000	1.00	1.00	0.9261
HA	0.395	1.000	1.000	1.000	1.00	1.00	0.8991
JH	1.000	1.000	0.671	1.000	1.00	1.00	0.9451
KA	1.000	0.973	1.000	1.000	1.00	1.00	0.9955
KE	0.995	1.000	1.000	1.000	1.00	1.00	0.9991
MP	0.820	0.605	0.492	0.761	0.765	0.764	0.7011
MH	1.000	1.000	1.000	1.000	1.00	1.00	1
OR	0.599	0.767	1.000	0.744	0.746	0.745	0.7668
PU	0.576	1.000	1.000	1.000	1.00	1.00	0.9223
RA	1.000	1.000	1.000	1.000	1.00	1.00	1
TN	1.000	0.921	0.968	1.000	1.00	1.00	0.9815
UP	0.589	0.644	0.592	0.895	0.897	0.896	0.7521
WB	0.885	0.700	0.716	0.882	0.892	0.894	0.8583
Grand average							0.8806

Table 4.4 INPTE of upper primary level of education for Special Category States (SCS) and Union Territories (UT) in India

State/UT	2005–06	2006–07	2007–08	2008–09	2009–10	2010–11	Average
AN	1.000	0.500	1.000	1.000	1.00	1.00	0.9166
ARP	1.000	1.000	0.507	0.764	0.765	0.766	0.8003
AS	0.940	0.738	0.588	0.825	0.827	0.829	0.7911
CHAN	1.000	1.000	1.000	1.000	1.00	1.00	1
DN	1.000	1.000	1.000	1.000	1.00	1.00	1
DD	1.000	0.521	0.894	0.667	0.669	0.676	0.7378
DE	1.000	1.000	1.000	1.000	1.00	1.00	1
HP	1.000	0.937	0.984	1.000	1.00	1.00	0.9868
JK	1.000	1.000	1.000	1.000	1.00	1.00	1
LAK	1.000	1.000	0.791	1.000	1.00	1.00	0.9651
MANI	0.603	0.414	0.422	0.452	0.454	0.456	0.4668
MEGHA	0.968	0.431	0.384	0.473	0.472	0.475	0.5338
MIZO	0.965	0.427	0.489	1.000	1.00	1.00	0.8135
NAGA	0.917	0.990	0.729	0.657	0.659	0.673	0.7708
PUDU	1.000	1.000	1.000	1.000	1.00	1.00	1
SI	1.000	1.000	1.000	1.000	1.00	1.00	1
TR	1.000	1.000	1.000	1.000	1.00	1.00	1
UTTA	0.649	0.434	0.487	0.617	0.649	0.637	0.5788
Grand average							0.8535

4.3.2.2 Input Oriented Technical Efficiency Score of Upper Primary Level of Education for Special Category States (SCS) and Union Territories (UT) in India

Table 4.4 depicts the estimated results of INPTE for SCS&UT upper primary level.

The figure presented in Table 4.4 reveal that for SCS&UT upper primary level, INPTE is equal to one for every year under the study for CHAN, DN, DE, JK, PUDU, SI, DN and TR. Although for AN, LAK and HP the level of INPTE is not equal to one for each of the year, for AN it was less than one only for one year 2006–07, for LAK it was less than one only for 2006–07 and 2008–09, for HP it was less than one only for 2006–07 and 2007–08. Therefore the level of INPTE for AN, LAK and HP are also sufficiently high. The INPTE level has declined over the years for ARP, AS, DD, MANI, MEGHA, NAGA and UTTA, while it has increased for MIZO. The INPTE is least for MANI. The grand average level of TE for all the States/UT and for all the years is 0.8535. The States/UT having TE higher than that of grand level are AN, CHAN, DN, DE, JK, HP, LAK, MIZO, PUDU, SI, TR, while the States/UT having INPTE below that of this grand average are ARP, DD, AS, MANI, MEGHA and UTTA.

4.3.3 *Radial and Slack Movements in Inputs*

4.3.3.1 Input Slack and Radial Movement in Case of Input Oriented Technical Efficiency Score (INPTE) at Primary Level of Education in India

The input oriented measure of technical efficiency considered in this chapter is basically the radial measure. Thus the States/UT that were fully efficient having INPTE equal to one have efficient and optimum utilization of all the inputs and thus their radial values are zero. But as argued in Chap. 2 there may be slack movement for the efficient States/UT and hence for the efficient States/UT the extent of underutilization is given by only the slack movement for the concept and measurement of input slack see also Ray (2004). The rest of the states have radial movement and or slack movement on the average for all the inputs, and the combined value of slack and radial movement gives a measure of their inefficient input utilization. The computed percentage of the ratios of average of the slack and radial movements to that of average of actual figure of the four inputs used by the different states over the time period 2005–06 to 2010–11, using input oriented DEA measure for different categories of state and for primary and upper primary level are represented in Tables 4.5, 4.6, 4.7 and 4.8.

Slack and Radial Movement for Different Inputs Computed Under INPTE Measure at GCS Primary Level of Education

The estimated results of Slack and Radial movement for different inputs computed under Input oriented Technical Efficiency measure at primary level of education and for GCS is presented in Table 4.5.

For GCS primary education level, INPTE is equal to one for every year for BI, KA and JH. The observed figure presented in Table 4.5 suggests that in case of GCS Primary level among the three technically efficient states BI, JH and KA, only in case of KA both radial and slack movement are zero. Thus although BI and JH are technically efficient and the observed output bundle lies on the frontier, however, one can reduce further some of the input level and can produce same level of output. This observation can be interpreted by saying that virtually we need less amount of input to produce the same level of output. For example, in case of BI there is 25 and 24.17 % input slack for the two input *teacher pupil ratio* and the *percentage of teachers with qualification graduate and above respectively*. Similarly, in case of JH the extent of input slack turns out to be 34.42 and 4.18 % for the two inputs: *number of primary school per lakh of population and the percentage of teachers with qualification graduate and above respectively*. A closer look at the Table 4.5 gives the following details regarding the radial and slack movements of the four inputs used in the production process.

For the input *school per lakh of population,* mean value of *radial movement* for the GCS primary group turned out to be 31.9723 %. The states having higher than

Table 4.5 Slack (S) and radial (R) movement for different inputs computed under INPTE measure for GCS primary level of education in India

States	No of primary schools per lakh population		Teacher-pupil ratio at primary		Classroom-student ratio at primary		% of teachers with qualification graduate and above at primary	
	R	S	R	S	R	S	R	S
AP	−19.3851	−9.37414	−19.375	−11.25	−19.1667	0	−19.3854	−17.9874
BI	0	−24.1726	0	−25	0	0	0	−24.1725
CHHA	−31.8217	−28.2094	−31.6667	−3.125	−31.6667	−10.625	−31.8213	0
GO	−25.4423	−9.7571	−24.875	−24.5	−25.25	−29.125	−25.4409	0
GU	−1.9381	0	−2.5	−10	−2.5	−10	−1.93818	−0.32087
HA	−32.9597	0	−33.3333	0	−33.3333	−6.66667	−32.9602	−8.01372
JH	0	−38.42	0	−30	0	0	0	−4.17693
KE	−0.1446	0	0	−1.875	0	−7.5	−0.14467	−2.1684
MP	−44.6801	−10.8141	−44.1667	0	−36.6667	−1.66667	−43.4657	−0.68547
MH	−56.534	−0.24333	−17.9167	−21.25	−13.3333	−10	−12.7336	0
OR	−48.3823	−42.26	−15.8333	−14.1667	−12.6042	−16.3542	−12.8072	0
PU	−75.9749	−20.560	−39.1667	0	−39.375	−18.75	−36.0513	−9.56977
RA	−85.24	−37.56	−40	0	−46.25	−22.0833	−36.4654	−21.193
TN	−1.3007	0	−1.66667	−0.83333	−1.25	−0.625	−1.30083	0
UP	−62.5052	−1.8258	−32.5	0	−32.5	0	−32.6118	−2.32988
WB	−25.28	−34.520	−27.5	−8.75	−17.625	−10	−18.2652	0
AVERAGE	−31.97	−92.534	−25.423	−13.705	−23.963	−11.950	−21.814	−9.062

Table 4.6 Input slack and radial movement taken together in case of INPTE measure for GCS primary level of education in India

States	No. of primary schools per lakh population	Teacher-pupil ratio at primary	Classroom-student ratio at primary	% of teachers with qualification graduate and above at primary
AP	−28.7592	−30.625	−19.1667	−37.3728
BI	−24.1726	−25	0	−24.1725
CHHA	−60.0312	−34.7917	−42.2917	−31.8213
GO	−35.1994	−49.375	−54.375	−25.4409
GU	−1.9381	−12.5	−12.5	−2.25905
HA	−32.9597	−33.3333	−40	−40.9739
JH	−38.4195	−30	0	−4.17693
KE	−0.14464	−1.875	−7.5	−2.31307
MP	−55.4943	−44.1667	−38.3333	−44.1512
MH	−56.778	−39.1667	−23.3333	−12.7336
OR	−90.6462	−30	−28.9583	−12.8072
PU	−96.5394	−39.1667	−58.125	−45.6211
RA	−122.80	−40	−68.3333	−57.6584
TN	−1.3007	−2.5	−1.875	−1.30083
UP	−64.331	−32.5	−32.5	−34.9416
WB	−59.48	−36.25	−27.625	−18.2652
Average	−48.0624	−27.6302	−28.4322	−24.75

mean value of radial movement are MP, OR, PU, RA and UP. The highest value *of radial movement* occurs for the state RA and least value occurs for TN. The mean value of *slack movement* for this input is 13 %. The States having slack movement greater than this average are WB, RA, PU, OR, JH, GO and BI. The slack movement is highest for OR and is least for MH.

For the input *teacher pupil ratio*, mean value of *radial movement* for the GCS primary group turned out to be 25.423 %. The States having higher than mean value of radial movement are CHHA, HA, MP, PU, RA, UP AND WB. The highest value *of radial movement* occurs for the state MP and least value occurs for TN. The mean value of *slack movement* for this input is 13 %. The states having slack movement greater than this average are BI, GO, JH, MH and OR. The slack movement is highest for BI and is least for CHHA..

For the input *class room student ratio*, the mean value of *radial movement* for the GCS primary group turned out to be 23.96 %. The states having *radial movement* higher than the mean are CHHA, HA, MP, PU, RA and UP. The highest value of *radial movement* occurs for the state RA and least value occurs for TN. The mean value of *slack movement* for this input is 11.95 %. The States having *slack movement* greater than this average are CHHA, GO, HA, MP, PU, RA and UP.

Table 4.7 Input slack (S) and radial (R) movement computed under input oriented technical efficiency measure for SCS and Union Territories (UT) primary level of education in India

States	No. of primary schools per lakh population		Teacher-pupil ratio at primary		Classroom-student ratio at primary		% of teachers with qualification graduate and above at primary	
	R	S	R	S	R	S	R	S
AN	−15.4116	−0.72885	−15.125	0	−15	−10.625	−15.4121	0
ARP	−43.0019	−31.9399	−42.6667	0	−42.875	−8.75	−43.0012	0
AS	−1.15939	−24.4	−0.625	−9.375	−1.25	0	−1.1602	0
DD	−3.9494	0	−3.75	0	−4.16667	0	−3.94961	0
DE	−1.339	0	−1.66667	−3.33333	−1.66667	0	−1.33874	0
HP	−11.3118	−1.13756	−11.25	0	−11.0714	−7.5	−11.3112	0
JK	−25.6961	−19.4154	−26	−3.5	−25.75	−7	−25.6959	0
MANI	−42.451	−12.7511	−42.5	0	−42.5	−5	−42.4506	0
MEGHA	−31.4161	−25.1709	−31.6667	−2.08333	−31.5	−4.58333	−31.4144	0
MIZO	−33.1164	−19.3663	−33.4167	−8.75	−33.1667	−20.5833	−33.1185	0
NAGA	−33.422	0	−33.625	0	−33.625	−3.5	−33.4219	0
PUDU	−6.99295	0	−6.66667	0	−6.66667	−7.5	−6.99302	0
SI	−9.47079	−9.47079	−9.375	−3.4375	−9.64286	−5	−9.47052	0
UTTA	−31.1729	−22.1753	−31.25	0	−31.25	−10.875	−31.173	0
Average	−20.708	−16.657	−20.681	−5.080	−20.724	−8.265	−20.708	0.000

Table 4.8 Input slack and radial movement taken together in case of INPTE measure for SCS&UT primary level of education in India

States	No. of upper-primary schools per lakh population	Teacher-pupil ratio at primary	Classroom-student ratio at primary	% of teachers with qualification graduate and above at primary
AN	−16.1404	−15.125	−25.625	−15.4121
ARP	−74.9418	−42.6667	−51.625	−43.0012
AS	−25.5694	−10	−1.25	−1.1602
DD	−3.9494	−3.75	−4.16667	−3.94961
DE	−1.339	−5	−1.66667	−1.33874
HP	−12.4494	−11.25	−18.5714	−11.3112
JK	−45.1115	−29.5	−32.75	−25.6959
MANI	−55.2021	−42.5	−47.5	−42.4506
MEGHA	−56.587	−33.75	−36.0833	−31.4144
MIZO	−52.4827	−42.1667	−53.75	−33.1185
NAGA	−33.422	−33.625	−37.125	−33.4219
PUDU	−6.99295	−6.66667	−14.1667	−6.99302
SI	−18.9416	−12.8125	−14.6429	−9.47052
UTTA	−53.3482	−31.25	−42.125	−31.173
AVERAGE	−32.600	−22.860	−27.220	−20.710

The *slack movement* is highest for GO and is least for TN. The *slack movement* is zero for the states AP, BI, JH and UP.

For the input *percentage of teacher with qualification graduate and above*, the mean value of *radial movement* for the GCS primary group turned out to be 21.81 %. The States having *radial movement* higher than mean value are CHHA, GO, HA, MP, PU, RA and UP. The highest value of *radial movement* occurs for the State MP and least value occurs for TN. The mean value of *slack movement* for this input is 9.602 %. The states having slack movement greater than this average are AP, BI, PU and RA. The slack movement is zero for the states CHHA, GO, MH, OR, TN and WB. The slack movement is highest for BI and is least for HA.

The estimation of this radial and slack movement is very crucial because they give some idea about the underutilisation of different inputs used in the production process. What ultimately is important is the extent of the underutilisation of any input, which can be measured by the sum of Slack and Radial movement taken together for that input. The estimation of this radial and slack movement will thus be used to derive the extent of underutilisation of different inputs used in the production process and to rank the inputs depending on the degree of underutilisation.

For GCS primary level of education such underutilization can be visualized from Table 4.6.

The figures presented in Table 4.6 suggest that if one consider the radial and slack movement taken together (R&S), *for the input school per lakh of population,* the average magnitude of R&S is 48.06 %. The States having R&S higher than this average are CHHA, MP, MH, OR, PU, RA, UP and WB. The extent of R&S is highest for RA and least for TN.

If one consider the radial and slack movement taken together (R&S), *for the input teacher pupil ratio*, the average magnitude of R&S is 27.63 %. The States having R&S higher than this average are AP, CHHA, GO, HA, JH, MP, MH, OR, PU, RA, UP and WB. The extent of R&S is highest for GO and least for TN.

For the input *classroom student ratio*, the average magnitude of R&S is 28.34 %. The States having R&S higher than this average are CHHA, GO, HA, MP, OR, PU, RA and UP. The extent of R&S is highest for CHHA, while it is lowest for TN.

For the input *percentage of teachers with qualification graduate and above*, the mean value of R&S is turned out to be 24.75 %. The States having R&S higher than this average are AP, CHHA, GO, HA, MP, PU, RA and WB. The extent of R&S is highest for MP, while it is lowest for TN.

Input Slack and Radial Movement Under Input Oriented Technical Efficiency Measure for Primary Level of Education Corresponding to Special Category States (SCS) and Union Territories (UT) in India

The estimated results of Slack and Radial movement for different inputs computed under Input oriented Technical Efficiency measure at Primary Level of Education and for Special Category States (SCS) and Union Territories (UT) in India GCS is presented in Table 4.7.

INPTE is equal to one for every year under the study for the States/UT like CHAN, LAK and TR. For the efficient states the radial movement must be zero but the slack movement for the efficient States/UT not necessarily always be zero. For the present case, the results of estimation suggest that slack movements for different inputs are zero also for the efficient states. Further, the slack movements are zero also for some of the inefficient states having nonzero radial movements. For example, the slack movements is zero in case of the inputs like (i) number of school per lakh of population for DD, DE, NAGA and PUDU, (ii) Teacher pupil ratio at the primary level, for AN, ARP, AS, HP, MANI, NAGA and PUDU, (iii) class room student ratio at primary level for AS, DD, DE and (iv) percentage of teachers with qualification graduate and above for all the States/UT. But in contrast to GCS primary group, none of efficient States/UT have non zero slack movements for any of the inputs.

A closer look at the Table 4.7 gives the following details regarding the radial and slack movements of the four inputs used in the production process corresponding SCS&UT primary level of education.

Considering SCS&UT primary level and for the input *the number of primary school per lakh of population*, it can be said that mean value of *radial movement* for the SCS&UT primary group turned out to be 20.708 %. The States/UT having *radial movement* higher than mean value of is ARP, JK, MANI, MEGHA, MIZO, NAGA and UTTA. The highest value of *radial movement* occurs for the state ARP and least value occurs for AS. Considering *slack movement* it can be found that the mean value of *slack movement* for this input for SCS&UT primary group turned out to be 16.657 %. The states having *slack movement* greater than this average are ARP, AS, JK, MEGHA, MIZO and UTTA. The *slack movement* for this input is zero for some of the inefficient States/UT like DD, DE, NAGA and PUDU; is highest for ARP and is least for AN.

For the input *teacher pupil ratio*, mean value of *radial movement* for the SCS&UT primary group turned out to be 20.681 %. The States having radial movement higher than mean value of are ARP, JK, MANI, MEGHA, MIZO, NAGA and UTTA. The highest value of radial *movement* occurs for the state ARP and least value occurs for AS. Considering *slack movement* of this input it can be found that the mean value of *slack movement* for this input is 5.08 %. For AS and MIZO *slack movement is* higher than this average. The slack movement for this input is zero for some of inefficient States/UT like AN, ARP, DD, HP, MANI, NAGA and PUDU; is highest for BI and is least for HA.

For the input *classroom student ratio*, mean value of *radial movement* for the SCS&UT primary group turned out to be 20.724 %. For ARP, JK, MANI, MEGHA, MIZO, NAGA and UTTA the extent of *radial movement* of this input is higher than its mean value. The radial movement is highest for ARP and is least for AS. Considering slack movement of this input it can be found that the mean value of *slack movement* for this input for the SCS&UT primary group is 5.447 %. The states having *slack movement* greater than this average are AN, ARP, MIZO and UTTA. The *slack movement* is highest for MIZO and is least for UTTA. Some of the inefficient States/UT like AS, DD and DE have zero slack movement for this input.

For the input *percentage of teachers with qualification graduate and above at primary*, mean value of *radial movement* for the SCS&UT primary group turned out to be 20.708 %. The states having *radial movement* higher than mean value of are ARP, JK, MANI, MEGHA, MIZO, NAGA and UTTA. The radial *movement* is highest for the state ARP and is least for DE. Considering *slack movement* of this input it can be found that it is zero for all the states belonging to SCS&UT at the primary level.

The extent of Slack and Radial movement taken together for different inputs under Input oriented Technical Efficiency measure at primary level of education and for SCS&UT is presented in Table 4.8.

Figures presented in Table 4.8 shows that if one consider the slack *and radial movement taken together* (R&S), *for the input number of upper primary school per lakh of population*, the mean value of R&S turned out to be 32.06 %. The States/UT having R&S higher than this average are ARP, JK, MANI, MEGHA, MIZO, NAGA and UTTA. The R&S for this input is highest for ARP and least for DE.

For the input teacher pupil ratio, the average value of R&S turned out to be 22.86 %. The States/UT having R&S higher than this average are ARP, JK, MANI,

MEGHA, MIZO, NAGA and UTTA. The extent of R&S for this input is highest for ARP and least for DD.

For the input classroom student ratio, the mean value of R&S turned out to be 27.22 %. The States/UT having R&S higher than this average are ARP, JK, MANI, MEGHA, NAGA and UTTA. The extent of R&S for this input is highest for ARP and least for AS.

For the input percentage of teachers with qualification graduate and above, the mean value of R&S turned out to be 20.71 %. The States/UT having R&S higher than this average are ARP, JK, MANI, MEGHA, MIZO, NAGA, PUDU and UTTA. The extent of R&S for this input is highest for ARP and least for AS.

4.3.3.2 Input Slack and Radial Movement Computed Under Input Oriented Technical Efficiency Measure Corresponding to Upper Primary Level of Education in India

Input Slack and Radial Movement Under Input Oriented Technical Efficiency Score for Upper Primary Level of Education Corresponding to General Category States (GCS) in India

The estimated results of Slack and Radial movement for different inputs computed under Input oriented Technical Efficiency measure at Upper Primary Level of Education and for GCS in India are presented in Table 4.9.

For GCS upper primary level, TE is equal to one for the States/UT like AP, BI, MH and RA. For BI there *is slack movement* of about 12 % for the input percentage of teachers with qualification graduate and above. This suggests that although BI is technically efficient, it is possible to reduce this input by 12 % and produce same level of output. Alternatively, we can interpret the result by stating that we need less amount of this input to produce the same level of output.

The figures presented in Table 4.9 also suggest that for the inefficient states having non-zero *radial movement* for different inputs, the *slack movement* is zero for some of the states. For example, the *slack movement* is zero for the inputs like (i) number of school per lakh of population corresponding to the states BI, GU, KE, MH, RA, TN and WB, of which fully efficient states are BI, MH, and RA. (ii) teacher pupil ratio, for BI, GO, HA, OR, TN, UP and WB of which fully efficient states is BI, (iii) class room student ratio for BI. KE and TN, of which technically efficient state is BI and (iv) percentage of teachers with qualification graduate and above corresponding to CHHA, KE, MP and UP. This in turn implies that some of the inefficient states have zero *slack movements* for this input.

A closer look at the Table 4.9 gives the following details regarding the *radial* and *slack movements* of the four inputs used in the production process corresponding to GCS upper primary level.

For the input *number of upper primary school per lakh of population*, at GCS upper primary level, mean value of *radial movement* turned out to be 20.373 %. The States having *radial movement* higher than this mean value are CHHA, GO,

Table 4.9 Input slack (S) and radial movement computed under input oriented technical efficiency measure for GCS upper primary level of education in India

States	No. of primary schools per lakh population		Teacher-pupil ratio at upper primary		Classroom-student ratio at upper primary		% of teachers with qualification graduate and above at upper primary	
	R	S	R	S	R	S	R	S
BI	0	0	0	0	0	0	0	−12.2281
CHHA	−43.0379	−48.3994	−42.75	−0.5	−43	−13.667	−43.0382	0
GO	−41.3792	−5	−41.4583	0	−41.125	−22.25	−41.3852	−7.71878
GU	−12.5	0	−12.5	−1.66667	−12.9167	−0.8333	−12.5027	−28.2013
HA	−15.1275	−16.7325	−15	0	−15	−5.4167	0	−6.69578
JH	−9.0875	−0.475	−9.16667	−18.6667	−9.16667	−32.083	−9.09102	−30.2825
KE	−0.125	0	0	−2.5	−0.11	0	−0.12424	0
MP	−34.6843	−53.5992	−35.4167	−5.83333	−34.9167	−13.5	−58.27	0
MH	0	0	0	−1.875	0	−8.125	0	−11.9738
OR	−22.5871	−44.8396	−22.9167	0	−22.9167	−17.5	−22.5872	−4.35138
PU	−10.6125	−43.8427	−10.8333	−32.5	−10.625	−6.25	−10.6122	−22.0209
RA	0	0	0	−25.5	0	−19.375	0	−28.3128
TN	−1.63036	0	−1.66667	0	−1.66667	0	−1.62972	−13.4135
UP	−33.6345	−48.5743	−32.5	0	−33.3333	−12.917	−33.633	0
WB	−20.075	0	−18.75	0	−19.25	−11	−20.069	−12.4152
Average	−20.373	−32.683	−22.087	−11.130	−22.175	−13.577	−16.66	−16.146

MP, OR and UP. The extent of radial movement is highest for CHHA, and is lowest for TN. Regarding *slack movement*, it can be said that the mean value of *slack movement* for this input is 32.683 %. The States having slack movement higher than this average are CHHA, MP, OR, PU and UP. The slack movement is highest for MP and is least for GO.

Considering the input *teacher pupil ratio*, it can be found that radial movement for this input is highest for the state MP and least for TN. The mean value of *radial movement* turned out to be 22.087 %. The States having *radial movement* higher than this mean are CHHA, MP, OR, PU and UP. Regarding *slack movement* it can be said that the mean value of *slack movement* for this input corresponding to GCS primary group is 11.13 %. The States having *slack movement* higher than this average slack are JH, PU and RA. The *slack movement* is highest for MP and is least for GO.

For the input *class room student ratio*, the mean value of radial movement for the GCS upper primary group turned out to be 22.175 %. The states having *radial movement* higher than this mean are GO, MP, OR and UP. The highest value of *radial movement* occurs for the state GO and least value occurs for TN. Considering *slack movement* for this input it can be said that it is zero for the States BI, KE and TN of which technically efficient state is BI.

For the input teacher *pupil ratio* the mean value of *slack movement* for this input is 13.57 %. The states having slack movement greater than this average are CHHA, GO, HA and RA. The *slack movement* for this input corresponding to the GCS upper primary group is highest for JH and is least for GU.

For the input *percentage of teacher with qualification graduate and above*, the mean value of *radial movement* for the GCS upper primary group turned out to be 16.66 %. The States having *radial movement* higher than this mean are CHHA, GO, OR, UP and WB. The highest value of *radial movement* occurs for the State MP and least value occurs for KE. Considering *slack movement* for this input it can be said that it is zero for the states of which technically efficient State is BI. This in turn implies that some of the inefficient States have zero *slack movements* for this input. Considering the *slack movement* of this input it can be found that the mean value of *slack movement* for this input for GCS upper primary group is 16.14 %. The states having slack movement greater than this average are GU, JH, PU and RA. The slack movement for this input corresponding to the GCS upper primary group is highest for JH and is least for OR.

The extent of underutilization of different inputs as measured by the slack and radial movement taken together for different inputs computed under Input oriented Technical Efficiency measure for GCS upper primary level of education is presented in Table 4.10.

The figures presented in Table 4.10 suggest that, if one considers slack and radial movement taken together (R&S), *for the input number of upper primary school per lakh of population*, the mean value of R&S turned out to be 42.162 %. The states having R&S higher than this average are CHHA, GO, MP, OR, PU and UP. The amount of R&S is highest for CHHA and least for TN.

Table 4.10 Input slack and radial movement taken together computed under input oriented technical efficiency measure for GCS upper primary level of education in India

States	No. of upper-primary schools per lakh population	Teacher-pupil ratio at upper-primary	Classroom-student ratio at upper-primary	% of teachers with qualification graduate and above at upper-primary
BI	0	0	0	−12.2281
CHHA	−91.4373	−43.25	−56.6667	−43.0382
GO	−46.3792	−41.4583	−63.375	−49.104
GU	−12.5	−14.1667	−13.75	−40.704
HA	−31.86	−15	−20.4167	−6.69578
JH	−9.5625	−27.8333	−41.25	−39.3736
KE	−0.125	−2.5	0	−0.12424
MP	−88.2835	−41.25	−48.4167	−58.27
MH	0	−1.875	−8.125	−11.9738
OR	−67.4267	−22.9167	−40.4167	−26.9386
PU	−54.4552	−43.3333	−16.875	−32.6331
RA	0	−25.5	−19.375	−28.3128
TN	−1.63036	−1.66667	−1.66667	−15.0432
UP	−82.2088	−32.5	−46.25	−33.6338
WB	−20.075	−18.75	−30.25	−32.4843
Average	−42.162	−23.714	−31.295	−28.70

For the input teacher pupil ratio, the average value of R&S is 23.74 %. The States/UT having R&S higher than the mean are CHHA, GO, JH, MP, PU, RA and UP. The total amount R&S is highest for PU and least for TN.

For the input classroom student ratio, the mean value of R&S turned out to be 21.15 %. The States/UT having R&S higher than this average are CHHA, GO, MP, OR, PU, UP and WB. The amount of R&S is highest for GO and least for TN.

For the input percentage of teacher with qualification graduate and above the mean value of R&S turned out to be 28.70 %. The states having R&S higher than this average are CHHA, GU, GO, MP, OR, PU UP and WB. The amount of R&S is highest for MP and least for KE.

Input Slack and Radial Movement Computed Under Input Oriented Technical Efficiency Measure for Upper Primary Level of Education Corresponding to Special Category States (GCS) and Union Territories (UT) in India

The estimated results of slack and radial movement for different inputs computed under Input oriented Technical Efficiency measure for upper primary level of Education corresponding to Special Category States (SCS) and Union Territories (UT) in India GCS is presented in Table 4.11.

Table 4.11 Input slack (S) and radial (R) movement computed under input oriented technical efficiency measure and for upper primary level corresponding to Special Category States (SCS) and Union Territories (UT) in India

States	No. of primary schools per lakh population		Teacher-pupil ratio at upper primary		Classroom-student ratio at upper primary		% of teachers with qualification graduate and above at upper primary	
	R	S	R	S	R	S	R	S
AN	−12.5	0	−12.5	−38.611	−12.5	−46.25	−12.5	−42.627
ARP	−18.392	0	−18.333	−23.284	−18.125	−2.5	−18.389	−15.833
AS	−27.055	−45.692	−26.667	−21.75	−26.25	−0.8333	−27.055	0
DN	0	0	0	−42.624	0	−38.974	0	−40.781
DD	−20.408	−12.653	−20.333	−3	−20	−20.833	−20.409	−24.336
DE	0	0	0	−24.167	0	−13.333	0	−31.276
HP	−0.7963	−2.6903	−0.625	0	−0.833	0	−0.7964	−11.767
JK	0	0	0	−51.746	0	−49.083	0	−47.895
LAKH	−10.45	−6.2167	−10.625	0	−10.83	−3.3333	−10.453	−0.5858
MANI	−53.577	0	−53.75	−9.6875	−53.66	−2.0833	−39.821	0
MEGHA	−44.033	−52.762	−43.964	−11	−44.21	−7.125	−44.0327	0
MIZO	−29.7956	−30.871	−39.2014	−14.375	−29.62	−9.375	−29.7957	0
NAGA	−22.0149	−19.6159	−22.0833	−7.9167	−22.5	0	−22.0157	−5.25474
PUDU	0	0	0	−11.5	0	−13.875	0	−11.6939
SI	0	0	0	−46.630	0	−64.783	0	−43.5698
TR	0	0	0	−8.9286	0	−2.5	0	−2.26148
UTTA	−45.0398	−41.3443	−45	0	−45	−18.75	−45.0394	−8.10811
Average	−25.824	−26.480	−26.644	−22.516	−25.77	−19.575	−24.574	−21.998

The figures presented in Table 4.11 suggest that for the States/UT like CHAN, DN, DE, JK, PUDU, SI and TR INPTE is equal to one for all the years under the study. However, the results of estimation suggest that although DN, JK, PUDU, SI and TR are technically efficient, there exists *slack movement* for different inputs for some of this efficient States/UT. For example there is non-zero *slack movement* for the inputs like *pupil teacher ratio* corresponding to the States/UT DN, JK, PUDU, SI and TR and for the input like *percentage of teacher with qualification graduate and above* corresponding to the States/UT DN, DE, JK, SI and TR.

A closer look at the Table 4.11 gives the following details regarding the *radial and slack movements* of the four inputs used in the production process corresponding to SCS&UT upper primary level.

Considering SCS&UT upper primary level and for the input *the number of primary school per lakh of population,* it can be said that mean value of *radial movement* for the SCS&UT upper primary group turned out to be 25.824 %. The States/UT having *radial movement* higher than this mean value of are AS, MANI, MEGHA, MIZO, and UTTA. The highest value *of radial movement* occurs for the MANI and least value occurs for HP. Considering the *slack movement* it can be found that the mean value of *slack movement* for this input corresponding to SCS&UT upper primary group turned out to be 26.480 %. The States/UT having *slack movement* for this input greater than this average value are AS, MEGHA, MIZO and UTTA. The *slack movement* is zero for AN, ARP, DN, DE, JK, MANI, PUDU, SI and TR of which the fully technically efficient States are DN, DE, JK, PUDU, SI, and TR. The *slack movement* is highest for MEGHA and is least for HP.

Considering SCS&UT upper primary level and *for the input teacher pupil ratio*, it can be said that mean value of *radial movement* for the SCS&UT upper primary group turned out to be 26.644 %. The States/UT having higher than mean value of radial movement are AS, MANI, MEGHA, MIZO, and UTTA. The highest value of radial movement occurs for MANI and least for HP. Considering *slack movement* it can be found that the mean value of *slack movement* for this input corresponding to SCS&UT upper primary group turned out to be 22.516 %. The States having slack movement greater than this average are AN, ARP, DN, DE, JK and SI The slack movement is zero for HP, LAKH and UTTA of which are not the fully technically efficient states implying that non efficient states can have zero slack movement. The slack movement for this input is highest for JK and is least for DN.

For the *input classroom student ratio*, mean value of *radial movement* for the SCS&UT upper primary group turned out to be 25.777 %. The States having *radial movement* higher than this mean value are AS, MANI, MEGHA, MIZO, and UTTA. The highest value of radial movement for this input occurs for the State MANI and least value occurs for HP. Considering the slack *movement* of this input it can be found that it is zero for NAGA and HP corresponding to SCS&UT and for the upper primary level, which are not the efficient States/UT, again suggesting that slack movement can be zero for non-efficient states as well. The mean value of *slack movement* for this input corresponding to SCS&UT and for the upper primary level is 19.57 %. The States/UT having *slack movement* higher than this average are AN, DN, JK and SI. The highest value of *slack movement* of this input corresponding to SCS upper primary level occurs for SI, while the lowest value occurs for TR.

For the input *percentage of teacher with qualification graduate and above*, it can be found that mean value of the *radial movement* for this input and for SCS&UT upper primary level is 24.574 %. The States/UT belonging to SCS&UT upper primary group and having higher than this average are AS, MANI, MEGHA, MIZO and UTTA. For SCS&UT upper primary level, the radial movement is highest for UTTA and is lowest for HP. Considering the *slack movement* of this input, it can be found that the mean value of *slack movement* for this input corresponding to SCS&UT upper primary level is 21.988 %. For AN, DN, DD, DE, JK and SI, slack movement for this input is greater than this average slack corresponding to SCS&UT upper primary level. The slack *movement* is highest for JK, and is lowest for NAGA. It is zero for AS, MANI, MEGHA, and MIZO implying that *slack movement* can be zero for non-efficient states as well.

The extent of underutilization of different inputs as measured by the Slack and Radial movement taken together for different inputs, computed under Input oriented Technical Efficiency measure at primary level of education and for SCS and for union territories (UT) is presented in Table 4.12.

Figures presented in Table 4.12 suggests that, if one considers slack and radial movement taken together (R&S), for the input *number of upper primary school per lakh of population*, the mean value of R&S turned out to be 45.08 %. The States/UT having R&S higher than this average value are AS, MANI, MEGHA, MIZO and UTTA. The extent of R&S is highest for AS and least for HP.

For *the input teacher pupil ratio*, the average value of R&S turned out to be 35.78 %. The States/UT having R&S higher than this average value are AN, ARP, AS, DN, JK, MANI, MEGHA, MIZO, SI and UTTA. The magnitude of R&S is highest for MEGHA and least for HP.

For the input *number of upper primary school per lakh of population*, the mean value of R&S turned out to be 45.08 %. The States/UT having R&S higher than this average value are AS, MANI, MEGHA, MIZO and UTTA. The amount of R&S is highest for AS and least for HP.

For the input *classroom student ratio*, the mean value of R&S turned out to be 33.95 %. The States/UT having R&S higher than this average value are AN, DN, DD, JK, MANI, MEGHA, MIZO, SI and UTTA. The extent of R&S is highest for SI and least for HP.

The estimation of radial and slack movements of different inputs used in the production process for primary and upper primary level and for different categories of states gives an idea about the underutilization of input. The underutilization of input can be measured by the extent of radial and slack movement taken together (R&S). *For GCS primary level and for SCS&UT upper Primary level* the underutilization of inputs is highest for the input like number of school per lakh of

Table 4.12 Input slack and radial movement taken together computed under input oriented technical efficiency score for Special Category States (SCS) and for Union Territories (UT) corresponding to upper primary level of education in India

States	No. of upper-primary schools per lakh population	Teacher-pupil ratio at upper-primary	Classroom-student ratio at upper-primary	% of teachers with qualification graduate and above at upper-primary
AN	−12.5	−51.11111	−58.75	−55.12708
ARP	−18.3917	−41.61706	−20.625	−34.22245
AS	−72.747	−48.41667	−27.0833	−27.05539
DN	0	−42.62443	−38.9744	−40.78089
DD	−33.0614	−23.33333	−40.8333	−44.74521
DE	0	−24.16667	−13.3333	−31.27156
HP	−3.48669	−0.625	−0.83333	−12.56315
JK	0	−51.74603	−49.0833	−47.89507
LAKH	−16.6667	−10.625	−14.1667	−11.03917
MANI	−53.5775	−63.4375	−55.75	−39.82141
MEGHA	−96.7944	−54.96429	−51.3393	−44.03274
MIZO	−60.6666	−53.57639	−39	−29.79569
NAGA	−41.6308	−30	−22.5	−27.2704
PUDU	0	−11.5	−13.875	−11.69392
SI	0	−46.63014	−64.7827	−43.56982
TR	0	−8.928571	−2.5	−2.261479
UTTA	−86.3841	−45	−63.75	−53.1475
Average	−45.083	−35.780	−33.950	−32.720

population, followed by class room student ratio, teacher pupil ratio and least for percentage of teacher with qualification graduate and above. *For GCS upper primary level* the underutilization is highest for the input percentage of teacher with qualification graduate and above followed by number of upper primary school per lakh of population, class room student ratio, and is least for teacher pupil ratio; while for *SCS&UT primary level* underutilization is highest for the input like number of primary school per lakh of population, followed by class room student ratio, teacher pupil ratio and least for percentage of teacher with qualification graduate and above. Therefore the extent of underutilization is highest for the input like number of school per lakh of population for all the categories except for GCS upper primary level. For GCS upper primary level, the extent of underutilization is highest for the percentage of teacher with qualification with graduate and above. The extent of underutilization is lowest for the input like percentage of teacher with qualification with graduate and above except for GCS upper primary level, for which the extent of underutilization is lowest for teacher pupil ratio.

4.4 Analysis of the Factors Behind the Variation in Input Oriented Technical Efficiency Scores of Primary and Upper Primary Level of Education in India

After obtaining INPTE a second stage panel regression is resorted to for finding out the determinants for GCS, SCS and primary and upper primary level of education separately. The four panels consists of INPTE score for (i) each of the 17 GCS States for primary and upper primary level and (ii) for 18 SCS and UT states for primary and upper primary level over the period 2005–06 to 2010–2011 along with the determinants variables for each of the panel. Different regressions are tried out. Description of the factors influencing TE score can be found in Table 3.1 of the Chap. 3.

To test for appropriateness of the assumption of fixed effect *vis. a vis.* the random effect panel model, Haussmann's specification test is performed for each of the regressions which strongly rejects the assumption of fixed effect model in favour of random effect model. To take into account heterogeneity among the regions, dummy for the three regions East (d1), West (d2) and South (d3) is included in the regression taking North as a benchmark.

Results of panel regression suggest that infrastructural variables, policy variables and school specific variables and also the state level macro aggregates are important

Table 4.13 Significant variables influencing INPTE of GCS primary

Variables	Coefficients	z-value	Goodness of fit of model
SCSCPGM	−0.004	−3.15	Wald Chi^2 = 176.43
STSCPGM	−0.016	−2.70	P > Chi^2 = 0.0000
AGMPG	0.273	2.28	
POPDEN	0.007	2.92	
GINI	−0.005728	−3.92	
PTHQN	0.2105913	4.86	
d3	0.3105913	3.84	

Table 4.14 Significant variable influencing INPTE of SCS&UT primary level of education

Variables	Coefficients	z-value	Goodness of fit of model
SCTHP	−0.004	3.18	Wald Chi^2 = 124.49
AGMPS	0.57019	2.12	P > Chi^2 = 0.0000
GBFTB	0.332	4.62	
d3	0.5088304	3.59	
d1	0.0001903	4.57	
SFTBPGM	0.6446	2.51	
Square of AGMPS	−0.3238	−2.84	
SVSHR	0.07	2.32	

in explaining TE score for both the primary and upper primary level of education and for GCS and SCS and UT.

4.4.1 Analysis of the Factors Behind the Variation in Input Oriented Technical Efficiency Scores of Primary Level of Education in India

The results of estimation of the factors influencing input oriented measure of technical efficiency for GCS, SCS and union territories primary level of education are presented in Tables 4.13 and 4.14 respectively.

4.4.1.1 Analysis of the Factors Behind the Variation in Input Oriented Technical Efficiency Scores (INPTE) of GCS Primary Level of Education in India

INPTE *first of all* depends on availability as well as utilization of central grant (AGMPG) showing sensitivity of INPTE with respect to policy variables. Greater availability of central grant facilitates higher utilization of different inputs used in the production process. *Secondly*, the relationship is nonlinear among different explanatory variable. For example, there exists interaction among (i) AGM variable and the percentage of single class room school (SCSCPGM), (ii) AGM variable and the single teacher school (STSCPGM), the sign of the coefficient of the interaction term in both the cases are negative, implying that increase in AGM reduces the prevalence of single class room school or single teacher school and in turn reduces INPTE. *Thirdly*, INPTE is also positively and significantly influenced by quality of para teachers. The number of para teachers with qualification graduate and above as a percentage of total number of teacher is positively related to INPTE, suggesting the role of human capital in promoting the level of INPTE. *Fourthly*, the state specific variable like inequality in the existing distribution of income as measured by gini coefficient (GINI) has a role to play in explaining INPTE. Higher the extent of inequality in the distribution of income, the probability that the access to education will be limited to fewer number of household is higher. As a result, the proportion of the family sending their child to school will be less and the probability of the consequent drop out will be high. All these factors will likely to have a negative influence on the utilization of different inputs and hence on the INPTE level. The other state specific variable which is important is density of population (POPDEN). Higher the extent of density of population, higher will be the extent of efficiency. It implies higher the value of POPDEN more the concentration of child population and hence economics of scale in-terms of provision of inputs results.

Apart from these factors, INPTE is also influenced by regional variability. The regional dummy d3 for south taking north as a base is positive and statistically significant, implying that southern region is more technically efficient than north.

4.4.1.2 Analysis of the Factors Behind the Variation in Input Oriented Technical Efficiency Scores (INPTE) of SCS&UT Primary Level of Education in India

For SCS&UT upper primary level, INPTE *first of all* depends on availability as well as utilizations of central grant (AGMPS variable). However, the relationship is nonlinear among different explanatory variable. For example, there exists joint interaction among the AGMPS and the proportion of students getting free text book (SFTBGM variable). The coefficient of AGMPS variable is positive and statistically significant implying that as AGMPS increases proportion of students getting free text book may increase which in turn can lead to an increase in INPTE. The coefficient of AGMPS is positive but the coefficient of the square of the AGMPS term is negative. This implies that there exists a optimum level of AGMPS up to which there exists positive effect of AGMPS on INPTE and after that the effect of AGMPS on INPTE falls. The other significant policy variable is the proportion of girls getting free text book as compared to boys in the primary school (GBFTB). *Thirdly*, the state specific variable like inequality in the existing distribution of income as measured by gini coefficient (GINI) has a role to play in explaining INPTE. The level of INPTE reduces with increase in GINI, the argument given for this is same as before. The other state specific variable which is important is the income generated from the service sector (SVSHR). It positively and significantly affects the level of INPTE. As income increases probability that the house hold will send their child to school increases which in turn can increase efficiency of existing inputs through better utilization through economics of scale in terms of provision of inputs. Apart from these factors, INPTE is also influenced by regional variability. Two regional dummies d3 for South and d1 for East taking North as a base is positive and statistically significant, implying that southern and the eastern regions are more technically efficient than north.

4.4.2 Analysis of the Factors Behind the Variation in Input Oriented Technical Efficiency Scores of Upper-Primary Level of Education in India

The results of estimation of the factors influencing input oriented measure of technical efficiency for GCS, SCS and union territories upper primary level of education are presented in Tables 4.15 and 4.16 respectively.

Table 4.15 Significant variables influencing INPTE of GCS upper primary level of education

Variables	Coefficients	z-value	Goodness of fit of model
SFTBUP	−0.005	−2.87	Wald Chi^2 = 143.03
GBFSUPGM	0.023	2.62	P > Chi^2 = 0.000
AGMUPG	0.25	2.76	
CBCUPGM	−0.030	3.14	
STSCUPGM	−0.052	2.91	
DRINKW	0.0141	4.20	
GINI	−0.05234	−2.94	

Table 4.16 Significant variables influencing INPTE of SCS&UT upper primary level of education

Variables	Coefficients	z-value	Goodness of fit of model
WBSUP	−0.007	−3.64	Wald Chi^2 = 132.59
AGMUPS	0.317104	3.15	P > Chi^2 = 0.000
WPBUPGM	−0.01637	−2.93	
POPDEN	0.023	3.57	

4.4.2.1 Analysis of the Factors Behind the Variation in Input Oriented Technical Efficiency Scores (INPTE) of GCS Upper-Primary Level of Education in India

For GCS INPTE first of all depends on availability as well as utilizations of central grant (AGMUPG), showing sensitivity of INPTE with respect to policy variables. Greater availability of central grant facilitates higher utilization of different inputs used in the production process. However, the relationship is nonlinear among different explanatory variable. For example, there exists interaction between AGMUPG and the variables like (i) the girls to boys getting free text book, (ii) classes in the bad condition and (iii) single teacher schools. The interaction term is positive in the first case and negative for the last two cases. The interpretation is that more availability as well as utilizations of central grant increases the proportion of girls to boys getting free text book and reduces the prevalence of classes in bad condition which in turn increases INPTE of different inputs used in the production process. All these will have some effect on the level of INPTE. The other policy variable which is important is the proportion of students getting free text books at the upper primary (SFTBUP). Secondly, the level of INPTE is also influenced by the prevalence of favorable infrastructure. For example, proportion of school having drinking water facility is a significant explanatory variable in fostering the level of INPTE. Finally, the level of INPTE is also negatively influenced by the State specific variable like existing inequality in the distribution of income. The argument is same as before.

4.4.2.2 Analysis of the Factors Behind the Variation in Input Oriented Technical Efficiency Scores of SCS&UT Upper-Primary Level of Education in India

For **SCS *upper primary level***, TE **first of all**, depends on the availability and utilization of central grant (AGMUPS). The coefficient of AGM is positive and statistically significant implying that greater availability of central grant facilitates higher utilization of different inputs used in the production process. However, there exists some degree of nonlinearity among the explanatory variables. For example, there exists interaction term between school without pucca building and AGMUPS (WPBUPGM), the coefficient of this variable is negative and statistically significant, suggesting that greater availability of central grant in fact reduces the incidence of school without pucca building. These findings supports that policy variables are important in explaining INPTE. Secondly, INPTE score is negatively influenced by existence of poor infrastructure. For example, proportion of upper primary schools without building has a negative influence on INPTE. Thirdly, the state specific variable like density of population (POPDEN) has a role to play in explaining input oriented TE.

4.5 Conclusion

This chapter estimates the input oriented technical efficiency INPTE of elementary level of education for General Category States (GCS), Special Category States (SCS) and Union territories (UT) of India over the period 2005–06 to 2010–11, using non parametric method of DEA and also explains for the determinants of such INPTE taking into account (i) some factors from poor infrastructure to see whether poor infrastructure inhibit the achievement of INPTE, (ii) some social indicator to investigate whether inclusion of the backward classes into the education system increases INPTE, (iii) some policy variable to test whether provision of more public facilities increases INPTE and also (iv) some state level macro aggregates like per-capita net State domestic product, income inequality, and number of persons below the poverty line to see to what extent the general environment of the State matters in explaining INPTE. The chapter also finds the extent of inefficiency in utilization of different inputs used.

The major findings of the paper can be summarized as follows First of all, not all the states show improved performance of INPTE score over the period 2005–06 to 2010–11. Secondly, most of the States/UT are not fully technically efficient in their input utilization. Thirdly, regarding underutilization of different inputs it can be said that for GCS primary. SCS&UT primary and SCS&UT upper primary level, the extent of underutilization of input is highest for number of school per lakh population and is lowest for percentage of teacher with qualification graduate and above. But for GCS upper primary the underutilization is highest for percentage of teacher with qualification graduate and above and is least for teacher pupil ratio. Fourthly,

INPTE for GCS, SCS&UT primary and upper primary level depends on the availability as well as utilization of central grant (AGM). Greater availability of central grant facilitates higher utilization of different inputs used in the production process, supporting the role of policy variable in explaining INPTE. The other significant policy variables are proportion of girls getting free text book to boy's in the primary school and proportion of students getting free text book. These variables positively influence INPTE of GCS primary and SCS&UT primary level respectively. Fifthly, the State specific variable like inequality in the distribution of income as measured by the Gini coefficient has a role to play in explaining INPTE. As inequality in the distribution of income increases the access to education will be limited to fewer number of people and the proportion of the household sending their child to school will be limited, which in turn has a negative effect on the utilization of resources. This observation is true for GCS primary and upper primary level. The important other state specific variables explaining INPTE are the income generated from the service sector and the density of the population. The income generated from the service sector is important in explaining INPTE for SCS&UT primary level, while density of population is important in explaining INPTE for SCS upper primary level. Sixthly, input oriented technical efficiency also gets influenced by infrastructural facilities. For example, in case of GCS primary level, INPTE is positively influenced by the number of schools having drinking water facilities, showing that the existence of favorable infrastructure will have a positive impact on TE. Similarly, in case of SCS upper primary, proportion of upper primary schools without building have a negative influence on INPTE showing prevalence of poor infrastructure can in fact has a negative effect on TE. Seventhly, there exists nonlinearity among the explanatory variables. For example, in case of GCS primary level, there exists joint interaction between the availability of central grant and (i) the proportion of primary school with single classroom, (ii) the proportion of primary school with single teacher, the interaction term being negative in both the cases, suggesting that availability of central grant reduces the prevalence of the school with single class room or single teacher and hence reduces INPTE. In case of SCS&UT primary level, there exists joint interaction between the availability of central grant and the proportion of students getting free text book. The greater availability of the central grant increases provision of free text book which in turn increases INPTE. Also for SCS&UT primary level, the coefficient of AGM is positive, but the square of AGM is negative, implying that there exists an optimum level of AGM up to which the positive effect of AGM is realized and after that the effect of AGM on INPTE is negative.

Finally, there exists regional variability. For the GCS primary level, the regional dummy D3 for South taking North as a base is positive and statistically significant, implying that southern region is more technically efficient than northern. For SCS primary level, two regional dummies d3 for south and d1 for east taking north as a base is positive and statistically significant, implying that southern and the eastern regions are more technically efficient than northern.

The following policy suggestions emerge from the analysis. The greater availability as well as utilization of Central grant will have a favorable effect on the input oriented technical efficiency. Greater availability of central grant facilitates higher utilization of different inputs used in the production process. The availability of Central Grant first of all has a direct impact and secondly it has indirect impact as felt through the joint interaction among different variables as discussed above. The other policy variables which can have a favorable effect on the input oriented technical efficiency are the increase in the number of student getting free text book, and also the increase in the proportion of girls to boys getting free text book. The quality of the para-teachers, i.e., the proportion of para-teachers with graduate and above is a significant positive determinant of INPTE. Thus the recruitment of the teachers with better quality is needed. Further since para-teachers are employed in the absence of full time teachers filling up of the vacant teachers post can also be helpful for increasing INPTE.

Also, there is a need to reduce the inequality in the distribution of income. The reduction in the inequality of the distribution of income will have a favorable effect on the input oriented technical efficiency. Further, different measures leading to increase in income from the service sector for different states can also lead to an increase in the input oriented technical efficiency level.

Reference

Ray SC (2004) Data envelopment analysis: theory and techniques for economics and operations research. Cambridge University Press, Cambridge

Chapter 5
The Summary and the Policy Suggestions

Abstract The summary results show most of the States/UT is technically inefficient considering both output-oriented technical-efficiency (OUTTE) and input-oriented technical-efficiency (INPTE). Also not all the States/UT depicts improved performance over the sample 2005–06 to 2010–11. Higher literacy-rate or educational-development-index does not imply better OUTTE. The extents of underutilization of inputs are estimated. The determinants of both OUTTE and INPTE vary between General-Category, Special-Category States and between primary and upper-primary level, highlighting importance of policy, infrastructure, State-specific and social-indicator variables. At policy level, both INPTE and OUTTE can be enhanced by increasing (i) the availability and utilization of central grant (AGM), (ii) the proportion of girls to boys getting free text book, para-teachers having qualification graduate and above, school with drinking water facility, SC teacher, (iii) State's service sectors income, population-density and by reducing (i) without-building school, (ii) inequality of income-distribution. OUTTE can further be stimulated by increasing percentage of (i) schools getting school-development-grant, having common-toilet, (ii) SC-enrollment and by reducing proportion of (i) single-teacher-school, (ii) single-classroom-school, and (iii) below the poverty line population. INPTE can also be enhanced by increasing the proportion of students getting free text book. Effect of AGM on INPTE also operates through its joint interaction with other variables. For SCS&UT-primary effect of AGM on INPTE is positive up to a limit Although employment of average input-bundle in SCS&UT-school produces less benefit as compared to GCS-school both for primary and upper primary, elasticity of OUTTE with respect to AGM is higher for SCS&UT-school.

This book *first of all*, assesses how efficient primary and upper primary education is across different states of India considering both output oriented and input oriented measures of technical efficiency (TE). The study covers the period 2005–06 to 2010–11 and all the states and union territories of India, which are categorized into two separate groups, namely: (i) General Category States (GCS); and (ii) Special Category States (SCS) and Union Territories (UT). It measures temporal variation

A. Ghose, *Efficiency of Elementary Education in India*,
SpringerBriefs in Economics, DOI 10.1007/978-81-322-3661-0_5

of TE of both primary as well as upper primary level of education over this period for all GCS, SCS&UT and also compares the performance of efficiency score of primary and secondary level of education. The major departure of this book is its approach to estimating TE, which does not use a single frontier encompassing all the twenty-eight states and seven UT, as is done in the available literature. Rather, this method assumes that GCS, SCS and UT are not homogeneous and operate under different fiscal and economic conditions. The non-parametric Data Envelopment Analysis (DEA) has been used for estimation of TE. *Secondly,* the group frontier and Meta frontier analysis has been carried out. The Meta frontier defines the frontier corresponding to all the 35 states and union territories taken together. In particular, Technology Closeness Ratio (TCR) is computed to find out the divergence of the group frontiers from the Meta frontiers. Technology-closeness-ratio (TCR) show whether, maximum educational–output producible from an input bundle by a school located in a particular group of State is as high as what could be produced if the school belongs to the other group. *Thirdly,* the book measures extent of underutilization of different inputs used under production process separately. *Fourthly,* it tries to answer whether the States/UT having the high values of literacy rate or the educational development index are also the State with high value of TE score. *Fifthly,* the book also explains the determinants of output and input oriented measures of technical efficiency. Finally, while finding out the determinants of efficiency, it intends to take into account (i) some factors from poor infrastructure to see whether poor infrastructure inhibit the achievement of TE, (ii) some factors from favorable infrastructure to see whether favorable infrastructure induces the achievement of TE, (iii) some social indicators to investigate whether inclusion of the backward classes into the education system increases TE, (iv) some policy variables to test whether provision of more public facilities increases TE and also (v) some state level macro aggregates like per-capita net State domestic product, income inequality, and number of persons lying below the poverty line to see to what extent the general environment of the state matters in explaining TE. Also, rather than using a composite index the present book attempts to find out the individual effect of the different explanatory variables. The earlier result that social and policy indicators are not significantly related to the efficiency improvement as reported in Chap. 2 may be due to the use of composite index. It is quite possible that some of the individual factors comprising of the composite variables are significant while the others are not. Separate regression is carried out for primary and upper primary level. *The relative sensitivity of the central-grant in explaining the efficiency performance of primary and upper-primary education of both GCS and SCS&UT is estimated, which can be used for judging the efficacy of central grant in promoting technical efficiency of these two groups and there is paucity of such estimation.*

Chapter 3 *which is* concerned with output oriented measures of technical efficiency (OUTTE) postulates the following observation on OUTTE for primary and upper primary level of education and for GCS and SCS&UT.

Not all the states are fully technically efficient. There exists high degree of variation of TE across different States/UT both at primary and upper primary level corresponding to GCS and SCS&UT.

For General Category States (GCS) and for primary level, KA is the only fully technically efficient State over all the years under the study. The grand average of the OUTTE for all the States and all the years is 0.7902. The states having OUTTE higher than this grand average are AP, BI, CHHA, GU, KA, KE, MH, OR, TN and WB. The level of OUTTE has declined over the year for the States BI, CHHA, GU, MH, OR, RA, TN and WB; has increased for HA and remained more or less stagnated for AP.

For the *Special Category States and union territories (SCS&UT) and for the primary level* OUTTE the fully efficient States over the period under study are CHAN, DN, LAK and TR. The grand average level of OUTTE for all the years and all the States is 0.8588. The states having higher level of OUTTE as compared to the grand average are AN, AS, CHAN, DN, DD, DE, HP, JK, LAK, PUDU, SI, TR and UTTA. The level of OUTTE has increased for AN, MANI, NAGA and UTTA, has declined for the states AS, DD, HP, MEGHA, MIZO, SI and remain more or less stagnated for ARP and PUDU.

For *GCS and upper primary level,* fully technically efficient states are AP and KE. The grand average level of OUTTE for all the years and all the GCS turned out to be 0.7708. The level of OUTTE is higher than the grand average level for AP, GU, JK, KA, MH, RA, TN and WB. The level of OUTTE has increased under the period of study for GO, GU, HA, JH, OR, PU, UP and WB, has declined for the states BI, CHHA, KA, MH, RA and TN and remain more or less stagnated for MP.

For SCS&UT and upper primary level, it is found that no States/UT is fully technically efficient. The grand average of the TE for all the States/UT under SCS&UT and all the years for upper primary level turns out to be 0.8731. The States/UT having higher level of OUTTE as compared to this grand average are CHAN, DN, DE, HP, JK, LAK, MIZO, NAGA, PUDU and TR. The level of OUTTE has increased over the years for the States AS and PUDU, declined for the States AN, ARP, CHAN, DN, DD, DE, HP, JK, LAK, MEGHA, MIZO, NAGA, TR and UTTA, while it has remained more or less stagnated for MANI.

The analysis of group frontier and Meta frontier suggests that the TCR value ranges from 0.9753 to 0.8721, signifying that the group classification in fact matters and on average, the maximum output producible from an input bundle by a school required within the region *is not almost as high as* what could be produced if the school could choose to locate anywhere in India.

TCR corresponding to GCS is high as compared to SCS&UT with respect to both primary and upper primary level of education. Thus, we are getting less benefit from the employment of average bundle of input in a school that is located in a SCS&UT as compared to a school belonging to a GCS.

The *group efficiency* for *GCS* is low as compared to SCS&UT both in case of *primary* and *upper primary*. Although both GCS primary and upper primary level are more close to Meta but *they possesses lower value of group efficiency, representing the higher degree of variability among them.*

SCS&UT upper primary has a high value of average group efficiency (0.86), but a relatively low value for average Grand efficiency (0.75) as compared to SCS&UT primary indicating that in this group almost all schools behave homogeneously and relatively poorly as compared to *SCS&UT Primary*!

Results of panel regression suggest that infrastructural variables, policy variables, school specific variables, also the State level macro aggregates are important in explaining OUTTE scores. This observation is true for both the primary and upper primary level of education and for GCS and SCS&UT. The result is different from the earlier result as reported in Chap. 2 that social and policy indicators are not significantly related to the efficiency improvement.

The output oriented technical efficiency (OUTTE) is *first of all* explained negatively by the prevalence of poor infrastructure, like (i) percentage of school without building for GCS and SCS&UT primary level, (ii) percentage of school with single teacher for GCS upper primary and SCS&UT primary level and (iii) percentage of school with single classroom for GCS primary level. *Secondly,* OUTTE score is also influenced by the availability of human capital. For example OUTTE score is positively influenced by the proportion of Para teachers in the primary school (PTHP) for GCS primary level, implying that the availability of Para teachers are definitely important and significantly contributing to the OUTTE score. For GCS upper primary level the quality of Para teachers i.e., the proportion of Para teachers with graduate and above among the total number of teachers is a significant determinant of OUTTE supporting the fact that not only the number of the para teachers but also their quality that matters. *Secondly,* favorable infrastructure has also some role to play. The OUTTE is explained positively by (i) percentage of school with drinking water facility for SCS&UT primary, GCS and SCS&UT upper primary level, (ii) percentage of school having common toilet for GCS upper primary and SCS&UT primary level. *Thirdly,* policy-variables are important in explaining OUTTE. For example, availability and utilization of central grant is a positive and significant determinant for all groups GCS and SCS&UT primary; GCS and SCS&UT upper primary. Similarly, percentage of girls to boys getting free text book is important for determining OUTTE of SCS&UT primary, while percentage of school received school development grant is important for determining OUTTE of GCS primary. *Fourthly,* OUTTE is also influenced by social indicator variables. For example in case of SCS&UT upper primary OUTTE score is positively influenced by proportion of SC teachers to total teachers (SCTHUP), proportion of SC enrolment to total enrolment (SCENUP) suggesting that inclusion of backward classes into the system in fact increases the efficiency score. *Finally,* OUTTE is also influenced by State specific macro aggregate, For example, proportion of people lying below the poverty line negatively influence OUTTE for GCS and SCS&UT primary. Extent of the inequality in the distribution of income negatively influences OUTTE for GCS and SCS&UT upper primary. Percapita income generated from the service sector is a positive determinant of OUTTE for GCS primary and GCS upper primary. Another state specific variable which positively and significantly affects OUTTE of SCS&UT upper primary level is the density of population. The results also support existence of regional variability. The states from West and South are technically more efficient than North for GCS primary and upper primary. The states from east and South are technically more efficient than North for SCS&UT primary level.

TE score of both GCS and SCS&UT and for primary and upper primary level of education are significantly related to availability as well as utilization of actual grant from Centre (AGM). The *elasticity of TE with respect to AGM is higher for the SCS&UT as compared to the GCS both in case of primary and upper primary level of education. Also elasticity of TE score is higher for upper primary as compared to primary both in case of GCS and SCS&UT.*

Chapter 4 estimates the input oriented technical efficiency score (INPTE) of elementary level of education and estimates the degree of underutilization of different inputs used in the production process for General Category States (GCS), Special Category States(SCS) of India and Union territories (UT) over the period 2005–06 to 2010–11 and also explains for the determinants of such technical efficiency.

The major findings of the Chap. 4 can be summarized as follows. *First of all,* not all the States show improved performance of INPTE over the period 2005–06 to 2010–11. *Secondly,* most of the States/UT is not fully technically efficient in their input utilization. *Thirdly,* regarding underutilization of different inputs it can be said that for GCS primary, SCS primary and SCS&UT upper primary level, the extent of underutilization of input is highest for number of school per lakh population and is lowest for percentage of teacher with qualification graduate and above. For GCS upper primary the underutilization is highest for percentage of teacher with qualification graduate and above and is least for teacher pupil ratio. *Fourthly,* regarding the factors influencing the behavior of INPTE it can be said that INPTE for GCS, SCS&UT primary and upper primary level depends on the availability as well as utilization of central grant (AGM). Greater availability of central grant facilitates higher utilization of different inputs used in the production process, supporting the role of policy variables in explaining INPTE. The other significant policy variable are the proportion of girls getting free text book to boy's in the primary school for GCS primary and proportion of students getting free text book for SCS&UT primary level. *Fifthly,* the state specific variable like inequality in the distribution of income as measured by the Gini coefficient has a role to play in explaining INPTE for GCS primary and upper primary level. As inequality in the distribution of income increases the access to education will be limited to less number of people and the proportion of the household sending their child to school will be limited, which in turn has a negative effect on the utilization of resources. The other State specific variables which are important in explaining INPTE are the income generated from the service sector for SCS&UT primary level and the density of the population POPDEN for SCS&UT Upper primary level. It implies higher the value of POPDEN more the concentration of child population and hence economics of scale in-terms of provision of inputs results. *Sixthly,* input oriented technical efficiency also gets influenced by infrastructural facilities. For example, in case of GCS primary level, INPTE is positively influenced by the number of schools having drinking water facilities, showing that the existence of favorable infrastructure will have a positive impact on INPTE. In case of SCS&UT Upper primary, proportion of schools without building has a negative influence on INPTE showing prevalence of poor infrastructure can in fact has a negative effect on INPTE. *Seventhly,* there exists nonlinearity among the explanatory variables. For example, in case of GCS primary level, there exists joint interaction between the variable AGM representing availability as well as utilization of central grant and (i) the proportion of primary school with single classroom, (ii) the proportion of primary school with single teacher, the interaction term being negative, the interaction term being negative in both the cases, suggesting that availability as well as utilization of central grant reduces the prevalence of the school with single class room or single teacher and hence reduces the INPTE. In case of SCS&UT primary level, there exists joint interaction between the availability of central grant and the proportion of students getting free text book. The greater availability of the central grant increases provision of free text book which in turn increases INPTE. Also for SCS&UT primary level, the coefficient of AGM is positive, but the square of AGM is negative, implying that there exists an optimum level of AGM up to which the positive effect of AGM is realized and after that the effect of AGM on TE is negative.

Finally, there exists regional variability. For the GCS Primary level, the regional dummy d3 for south taking north as a base is positive and statistically significant, implying that southern region is more technically efficient than north. For SCS&UT primary level, two regional dummies d3 for south and d1 for east taking north as a base is positive and statistically significant, implying that southern and the eastern regions are more technically efficient than north.

The following policy suggestions emerge from the analysis. The greater availability as well as utilization of Central grant will have a favorable effect on both the output and input oriented technical efficiency. Greater availability of central grant facilitates higher utilization of different inputs used in the production process. The availability of Central Grant first of all has a direct impact and secondly it has indirect impact as felt through the joint interaction among different variables as discussed above. The other policy variables which can have a favorable effect on the input oriented technical efficiency are the increase in the number of student getting free text book, and also the increase in the proportion of girls to boys getting free text book. There is the need to provide school development grant. Further, there is also the need to reduce the presence of poor infrastructure like single class room school, single teacher school, without building school. Also, there is a need to reduce the inequality in the distribution of income. The reduction in the inequality of the distribution of income will have a favorable effect on the input oriented technical efficiency. Further, different measures leading to increase in income from the service sector for different States can also lead to an increase in the input oriented technical efficiency level. Increasing the proportion of schools with toilet and drinking water facilities can also help to improve technical efficiency level. The quality of the para-teachers, i.e., the proportion of para-teachers with graduate and above is a significant positive determinant of technical efficiency. Thus, the recruitment of the teachers with better quality is needed. Since para-teachers are employed in the absence of full time teachers filling up of the vacant teachers post can also be helpful for increasing technical efficiency.

FSC
www.fsc.org
MIX
Papier | Fördert gute Waldnutzung
FSC® C083411

Kolibri 360 GmbH
Ferdinand-Jühlke-Straße 7
99095 Erfurt, Deutschland
produktsicherheit@kolibri360.de